I0653234

Embroidery

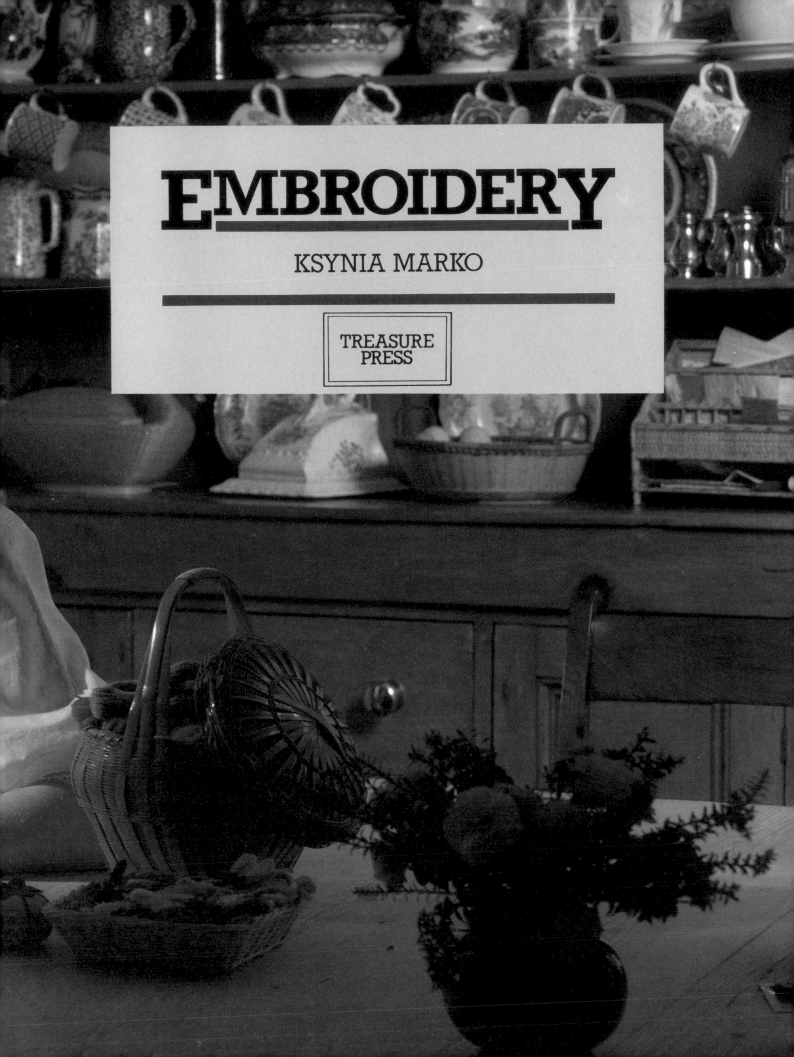

EMBROIDERY

KSYNIA MARKO

TREASURE
PRESS

NOTES FOR AMERICAN READERS

Throughout this book, the American term (where it differs from
the British one) is given in square brackets.

First published in Great Britain in 1982 by
Octopus Books Limted

This edition published in 1986 by
Treasure Press
59 Grosvenor Street
London W1

© 1982 Octopus Books Limited

ISBN 1 85051 141 1

Printed in Hong Kong

CONTENTS

HISTORY

Embroidery is one of the oldest of all crafts. From earliest times, when all cloth was hand-woven—often from undyed yarn—people have found various ways of embellishing it. Throughout the world different cultures have developed their own distinctive patterns and techniques, so that today the word 'embroidery' conjures up a wealth of styles: the delicate, subtly shaded pictorial work of the Chinese, the beadwork and quillwork of the North American Indians and the crisp whitework of the Swiss—to name only a few.

Like other crafts, however, embroidery is not practised in isolation. The opening of new trade routes in Europe and the East, and advances made in the fields of art and science, resulted in an exchange of decorative styles, materials and techniques. A striking example of this is the bold, colourful patterns of late 17th-century English crewel work, which was inspired by patterned chintz fabrics brought back from India by European merchants. Later, these embroideries were exported to India where they, in turn, inspired a type of Indian embroidery featuring swirling lines of chain stitch in many colours. Today, with our vastly improved communications, ease of travel and colour photography, we have access to innumerable traditions of embroidery, as well as to the experimental work of modern embroiderers who are developing this ancient craft in exciting new ways.

MEDIEVAL EMBROIDERY

To trace the entire history of embroidery in its myriad forms would require several large volumes. Here, however, we can sketch some of the main developments in the Western European tradition—a tradition that eventually took root in the New World also.

The end of the Dark Ages—in which merely surviving had occupied the energies of nearly everyone from prince to peasant—was attended by a flowering of all the arts and crafts, including embroidery. Perhaps the most famous example of early medieval needlework is the Bayeux Tapestry. This is not a tapestry at all, but an embroidery in wool on linen cloth depicting the Norman invasion of England in 1066. Measuring some 70 metres (230 feet) in length and half a metre (20 inches) in depth, it is crammed with detail and incident, from the sighting of Halley's Comet to Harold's death on the battlefield of Hastings. The origins of the Bayeux Tapestry are uncertain. It may have been commissioned by Bishop Odo of Bayeux, the half-brother of William the Conqueror, and the work may have been done by some of the professional English embroiderers already established in Canterbury and other cities. These embroiderers included men as well as women. In fact the design was almost invariably done by a man—a practice that was to continue until modern times.

Although embroidery was practised by aristocratic and royal ladies and also by nuns, it was considered too important to be left to amateurs, and workshops of professional embroiderers were established throughout Europe. There was a great demand for elaborate work to adorn the trappings of knights and kings; and the Church, in particular, needed splendid regalia that would help to proclaim the glory of God to the faithful.

It was in response to this need that the type of embroidery called Opus Anglicanum ('English work') was created. Produced by embroiderers in well-organized workshops, mainly in London in the 13th and 14th centuries, it used silk and metal threads and the finest stitching techniques to portray scenes

Above: American 18th-century sampler; Opposite: Portrait of Elizabeth I, splendidly dressed in an embroidered gown, richly worked in gold thread and encrusted with pearls.

from the Bible and the lives of the saints. The style was similar to that in contemporary manuscript illumination. Fine split stitch was used to delineate the intricate patterns and create subtle modelling effects. Areas of gold and silver couched work gave the vestments a shimmering appearance. Much of this was done in the technique called underside couching, in which the fine thread used to hold the thicker couched thread is pulled with each stitch, thus bringing the couched thread to the underside of the fabric at that point. On the right side none of the couching stitches are visible, and the metal threads look as if they are sewn through the fabric.

Not surprisingly, proficiency in these techniques was achieved only after a rigorous apprenticeship of seven years. High standards were maintained in embroidery—as in other crafts—by the craft guilds. Work was not allowed to be done in poor light, and any professional producing work of poor quality could be heavily fined or imprisoned.

The development of European embroidery received a temporary setback in the mid-14th century with the Black Death, which decimated Europe's population and had a disastrous effect on its economy. Also, the Hundred Years War (1337–1453) between England and France and civil unrest in England contributed to the decline of Opus Anglicanum in particular. New styles of embroidery, more attuned to an increasingly secular society, were soon to emerge.

THE RENAISSANCE

The Renaissance saw a shift in emphasis from church embroidery to embroidery as a status symbol for princes and nobles. Court costume for both men and women was richly encrusted with stitchery worked in silk, gold and silver threads, often studded with pearls and precious stones. The weight of the embroidery, added to that of heavy fabrics such as velvet, made some costumes so heavy that the wearers could scarcely move in them. Little of this magnificent work now remains, for when garments became unfashionable the jewels were removed. But we can gain some idea of its splendour from contemporary written accounts and from portraits.

Those of Queen Elizabeth I, in particular, show Renaissance embroidery at its most sumptuous. The Queen's taste for elaborate clothes (which symbolized her role as the personification of England's new power) was acknowledged in the numerous items of embroidery included in the gifts she received at the New Year. They included gowns, petticoats, sweet bags and gloves. On New Year's Day 1578, for example, Sir Philip Sidney gave the Queen a cambric chemise embroidered with blackwork and a pair of ruffs set with spangles. Blackwork, which is of Spanish origin, inspired by Moorish designs, was extremely popular in 16th-century England. Worked on white fabric, it combined regular, counted-thread filling stitches and the swirling floral designs characteristic of many other types of 16th-century embroidery. English blackwork was noted for its variety of stitch patterns and the frequent addition of gold threads to produce a richer effect.

A PASTIME FOR LADIES

From the Renaissance onwards, embroidery as a pastime became increasingly popular. This was particularly true in England. Under the Tudors the country was once again settled and prosperous and there was an expanding market for fine craftsmanship, including embroidery. Although many of the embroidered furnishings that adorned Tudor manor houses were worked by professionals, other pieces were embroidered by the mistress of the house, assisted by relations and servants. Embroidery was (and is) a sociable activity and it served a very practical purpose. A well-appointed household required a great number of furnishings, including bed curtains and coverlets, linens, wall hangings and cushions for stools and chairs.

Working the embroidery for these items was a full-time occupation, for the fashion—especially in the late 1500s—was for elaborate, complex designs. Floral patterns predominated, inspired by the new passion for gardens. Formerly confined to monasteries, gardens were now a feature of large private houses, and new species of flowers were imported and cultivated with enthusiasm. Tulips, hyacinths, marigolds, poppies, pinks, irises, sunflowers, nasturtiums and other blooms appeared in great profusion in Elizabethan embroideries, usually arranged within interlacing patterns of coiling stems.

Books of patterns intended for needlework began to appear in Europe in the 16th century. The design was transferred to the fabric by the 'prick and pounce' method, in which a fine powder (pounce) is rubbed through tiny holes following the lines of the design. An English book of patterns entitled *The Schole-house of the Needle* was published in 1624 and included instructions for altering the size of the designs. A later book, using patterns first published in Germany, featured some verses by the 'water poet' John Taylor announcing the range of subject matter:

Flowers, plants and fishes, beasts, birds, flies and bees,
Hills, dales, plains, pastures, skies, seas, rivers, trees,
There's nothing near at hand or farthest sought
But with the needle may be shaped and wrought.

Great households often employed a professional embroiderer, who copied designs onto the fabric and also instructed the ladies of the house in the finer points of stitchery. One such professional was engaged by Bess of Hardwick, Countess of Shrewsbury and the foremost needlewoman of Elizabethan times. In addition to providing designs for Bess's numerous projects, he probably worked some of the embroidery himself.

Ladies who did not require—or could not afford—a resident professional embroiderer might take or send cloth for a large project to the studio of a pattern-drawer.

SAMPLERS

Embroidery in the 16th and 17th centuries was almost always used on functional articles—clothing or furnishings. An exception to this rule was the sampler. A sampler was usually worked by a young girl as part of her education. Whatever her station in life, a girl was expected to be skilled in needlework, if only in plain sewing. Among more leisured families, embroidery of various kinds was added to the curriculum, and little girls laboured to perfect intricate stitches and expand their repertoire of motifs. The sampler served to record these achievements. A girl might work several samplers, one for each of the main types of surface embroidery and one for canvas work. She would then keep these handy for reference when planning and working her trousseau and later projects.

The samplers of the 17th century are particularly impressive. Some of them are a metre (yard) or more in length. The rows of designs become progressively more elaborate towards the end, where the worker's name and the date appear. They are rich in both patterns and stitches and must have occupied a child for many months.

By the 18th century the sampler had changed in both shape and content. The disciplined, regular patterns and inventive stitchery had been replaced by something more nearly resembling a picture, with a flowery border within which was worked a collection of single, charming motifs in a variety of stitches, along with biblical texts and pious poetry.

THE 18th CENTURY

In both England and the American Colonies—where growing prosperity and leisure were encouraging the needle arts—the 18th century witnessed a great vogue for crewel work. Although the word 'crewel' can be applied to any embroidery in wool thread on a background fabric, it usually refers to the swirling, brightly coloured patterns on cream-coloured linen

An 18th-century embroidery worked in long and short stitch.

typical of that age. Foliage, flowers, birds and butterflies mingle gracefully in this work. The most popular subject was the 'Tree of Life', a tree bearing all sorts of exotic, fanciful leaves and blooms. Chain and stem stitch were generally used for outlines and for stems and tendrils. The shapes might be filled in with trellis work or some other stylized filling, or more realistically with satin stitch or long and short stitch. Long and short—a difficult stitch to work smoothly—permitted subtle shading effects, giving added richness and depth to the design.

Shading was a highly esteemed skill in the 18th century. The highly stylized motifs of earlier times were giving way to realistic representations of flowers and other natural objects. A professional embroiderer was expected to have some knowledge of the principles of drawing from life. An article in a journal called *The London Tradesman* criticizes English embroiderers for being less inventive and skilled than their counterparts in France and Italy and states that an embroiderer 'ought to have a taste for designing, and a just notion of the principles of light and shade, to know how to arrange their colours in a natural order, make them reflect upon one another, and the whole to represent the figure in its proper shade'.

THE MACHINE AGE

Although amateur embroiderers usually chose their own stitches and colours, they did not feel free to create their own designs. Skill, not originality, was the goal. A new source of patterns was the magazine. In England, *The Ladies' Magazine*, first published in August 1770, offered its readers a 'free' needlework pattern with each issue—a now-familiar gimmick that greatly helped sales. The patterns, printed on long pull-out pages, must have been widely used; few have survived. The same idea was adopted in the 1830s by the new American publication *Godey's Lady's Book*.

From these beginnings developed not only the numerous embroidery patterns offered in modern magazines but also the leaflets and books published by embroidery thread manufacturers such as DMC and Coats to promote their own products.

With a seemingly inexhaustible supply of patterns and plenty of mass-produced materials available, the 19th-century embroiderer could set to work with enthusiasm—and she did. This was the era in which everything in sight was decorated. In embroidery, as in other decorative arts, the quality of design deteriorated. However, the period was not entirely one of stagnation, for whitework in general improved in quality and broderie anglaise [eyelet lace] was introduced. But the emphasis in most needlework was on quantity rather than quality.

The sewing machine—a boon to the dressmaker—also began to take on some of the decorative stitchery formerly done by hand. Ultimately this would have two beneficial results: it would free the needlewoman to do more imaginative work and eventually develop hand embroidery as an art form; also, the machine itself would prove capable of spontaneous, exciting embroidery at the opposite extreme from the dull, repetitive patterns it was first programmed to produce.

THE CRAFTS REVIVAL

But such innovations were a long way off in the 1860s, when the English designer and craftsman William Morris launched a movement to raise the quality of design in all the decorative arts. Morris began by designing embroideries, which he sometimes worked himself, though he is today best known for his textiles, wallpaper and book designs. The freshness and vitality of his designs had a liberating effect on English taste, and his attitudes and those of his followers in the Arts and Crafts Movement inspired a reawakening of respect for craftsmanship generally.

At about the same time, in 1873, the Royal School of

'The Artichoke' embroidered hanging, by William Morris, 1877.

Needlework was founded in London. It, too, represented a reaction against the products of the machine age, as well as an affirmation of embroidery as an art. Today it continues to keep alive the tradition of fine workmanship inherited from many centuries. Professional embroiderers at the School produce commissioned work, especially for ceremonial functions, and painstakingly repair work done in earlier times.

The fine stitchery and wealth of techniques inherited from her predecessors can be a great source of inspiration to the modern embroiderer, whether amateur or professional. Equally, she can look for inspiration—as embroiderers have always done—to other decorative and fine arts, such as jewellery, ceramics and painting, and transform ideas found there into material appropriate to her own medium. But the most stimulating source of all may well be the work of other modern embroiderers. For today embroidery is developing in all sorts of directions, with an exuberance and an innovative spirit never before seen. Professional embroiderers—a new breed of artist-craftsmen—are producing work of often startling originality, combining old techniques with new forms and sometimes incorporating such unlikely materials as paper and plastics to enlarge even further the meaning of the word 'embroidery'. And amateur workers are being encouraged to move on from ready-made patterns to creating their own designs. The enormous, constantly expanding range of styles and techniques offers limitless possibilities to anyone with a feeling for colour, shapes and texture.

MATERIALS
AND EQUIPMENT

The range of embroidery materials and equipment now available is virtually limitless. With experience you will learn which fabrics, threads and techniques you most enjoy working with, and which tools are most satisfactory to use. The projects in this book have been chosen to give you an idea of the scope of embroidery, so that you can discover and develop your own preferences and talents.

Embroidery need not be an expensive craft if care is taken in the choice of materials and their application. The beginner can practise techniques and experiment using interesting fabrics salvaged from old clothes, furnishings and remnants. Apart from silk and gold threads, most embroidery materials are not costly and you will find it well worth while to buy good-quality materials, especially for a project that will involve a lot of painstaking work. Time and energy will be wasted if you use poor-quality ground fabric and threads. Even a sampler of stitches will benefit from being worked with carefully chosen materials, which will induce you to take that little bit more pride in your work.

The basic hardware of frames and good tools may seem expensive, but once purchased will last for life.

FABRICS

Embroidery can be worked on any pliable material from chiffon to leather. The enormous range of both synthetic and natural fabrics can, in fact, be rather daunting to the beginner. Many synthetic fabrics have the advantage of being cheaper and more durable than natural fabrics, but in general they are more difficult to handle, and are best avoided until you have gained some experience using natural fabrics.

Some techniques, to be successful, require a specific type and quality of fabric. Crewel work should be done on a fabric strong enough to take the weight and thickness of wool, either the traditional linen twill or a furnishing fabric; whereas shadow work calls for one which is semi-transparent, so that the underside of the stitch can be seen. Blackwork and other types of counted thread embroidery need an evenweave fabric: one in which the number of warp and weft threads per centimetre (or inch) are equal.

The purpose of the embroidered object will also impose certain restrictions on the choice of materials and the way of working. Soft furnishings require materials which will survive frequent cleaning or laundering and techniques that will withstand a certain amount of wear. For example, fabrics that have long, floating threads in the weave, or are decorated by open stitches such as herringbone and fly stitch, will prove unsuitable for chair covers and cushions, as they may be snagged or distorted. If you find it difficult to choose a fabric for a functional object, a search around a department store looking at commercially produced articles may provide ideas. Attractive and interesting fabrics may in themselves be the inspiration for designs.

Embroidery on clothing may present special problems. A garment needs to be washed or dry cleaned fairly often, whereas embroidery needs as little handling as possible. One solution is to embroider motifs separately and hand-sew them lightly to the garment so they may be removed when the garment is cleaned. This gives you more options in choosing fabrics for the garment, and also permits the use of sequins, beads, metal threads and other fragile materials.

THREADS

Embroidery can be worked in many different kinds of thread— silk, cotton, linen, wool, synthetics and metal—in various weights and thicknesses. The distinctive qualities of each— from the lustre of silk to the soft, hairy texture of wool—create strikingly different effects. A piece of embroidery may be worked entirely in one type of thread, or it may combine several different types to create pleasing and exciting contrasts. The basic principle is that the thread and fabric should be in sympathy with and complement one another.

As in choosing fabric, you should bear the purpose of the article in mind. Silk floss on a frequently used furnishing item, for example, will not stand the wear and tear. If the thread causes unsightly distortion of the fabric, it is probably too thick or heavy. If it is so fine that the stitchery gets lost, a heavier thread or finer fabric is needed.

Some of the most common embroidery threads are:
crewel and tapestry wool
coton à broder
pearl cotton
stranded cotton [embroidery floss]
soft embroidery cotton
silk floss
twisted buttonhole silk

Ordinary sewing or tacking [basting] thread may be used in transferring a design (see page 37), and button thread is used for framing up and lacing work over cardboard (see pages 15 and 17).

NEEDLES

The needle is such a simple tool, yet without it embroidery would be impossible. The steel needles which we know so well were introduced in the 16th century and have become finer as technological advances have been made in their manufacture. There are a range of types, sizes and gauges now available which have been developed for specific uses.

Sharp	small round eye to take a single thread, pointed tip. Used mainly for dressmaking.
Crewel	long eye, slender, pointed tip
Chenille	long eye, shorter than crewel, larger range of sizes, pointed tip
Tapestry	long eye, blunt tip
Beading	very long, fine and flexible
Darning	similar to crewel
Curved	large- and small-eyed, half circle curve. Used mainly for upholstery.

When choosing a needle consider how it will be used. The thread or threads should pass easily through the eye. The needle should make a hole in the fabric large enough for the double thickness of thread, so that no effort is required when pulling it through. Crewel needles serve most general embroidery needs. The larger-eyed but shorter chenille needles may be easier to thread for people with less than perfect eyesight, while tapestry needles with their blunt tips are useful for woven stitches, as they do not split or pick up unnecessary threads. To avoid re-threading you can instead use the eye end of a pointed needle (see Pekinese stitch on page 19). Curved needles are extremely useful in the mounting and finishing of embroidered panels.

TOOLS

A pair of embroidery scissors with sharp, pointed little blades is essential. These will cut thread neatly, making it easy to insert in the needle. They are also useful in cutwork, enabling you to cut fabric close to stitchery with greater accuracy. For cutting large pieces of fabric you will need a good pair of sharp, dressmaking shears. In addition, you should have a pair of ordinary scissors kept specially for the cutting of paper.

Thimbles and magnifying glasses are an absolute necessity for some and unecessary for others. A magnifying glass may prove useful when working with metal threads or doing very fine work. It should be the type that hangs around the neck horizontally, with a base designed to lie against the chest. A thimble helps when working stitches with a sewing—as opposed to an up-and-down—movement. It should fit the finger snugly, so holding the needle steady as it is pushed through the fabric.

Ideally, all pins should be stainless steel to avoid any risk of marking the fabric. The T-shaped pins used by insect collectors are extremely useful for very fine fabrics. Both pins and needles should be stored in sand- or sawdust-filled pincushions to prevent rusting and to keep them sharp.

For drawing and transferring designs onto the fabric you will need a ruler and tape-measure, pencils and marking pen, French chalk, graph paper, tracing paper and dressmaker's carbon paper.

For couching metal threads a cake of beeswax is required; this is used for waxing the thread used to sew down the metal threads, to prevent its being cut by them. For beadwork you will need a small felt- or velvet-covered board for sorting the beads and pearls (see page 40).

Once an embroidery has been framed up and work started it is advisable to protect it with a clean cover-cloth. This should be slightly bigger than the frame and can be made from an old white sheet. If dyed fabric is used, make sure the dye is colourfast to avoid the risk of marking the work. Alternatively, the frame can be covered with white, acid-free tissue pinned to the fabric. If a frame is to be transported, it should be placed for protection in a strong, waterproof bag made from PVC [plastic-coated] fabric.

FRAMES

Many people can cope well without a frame but certain stitches and techniques, such as laid and couched fillings and metal thread work, can only be worked on a firm foundation—preferably one which is supported and so leaves both hands free to control the threads. In this way you can achieve a more professional result than by working in the hand and, once you have mastered the use of the frame, working will prove easier and more comfortable. The type of frame you choose will depend largely on the size and type of embroidery, the fabric used, and whether or not you want the work to be portable.

Many items, such as decorative panels employing free embroidery or gold work, are best worked in a frame on two layers of fabric, the lower, supporting layer being of a light to medium weight preshrunk linen or cotton. The object will be more durable and stitches neater and more even. Shadow work, drawn thread, pulled fabric and cross stitch embroidery are among techniques worked on a single piece of fabric requiring no extra support. The choice of whether or not to use a backing fabric will influence the method of working.

Round Frames

Round frames are the simplest type of frame to use, consisting only of two hoops placed one inside the other, trapping the material between them. The outer hoop can be tightened by means of a screw at the side. They are made of wood (or sometimes metal for machine embroidery) in various sizes, and some models can be attached to a floor or table stand or clamp.

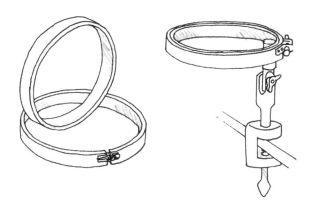

The advantage of a round frame is that its size and ease of mounting make it easily portable and usable even when travelling—one reason why it is so popular. The round frame is also extremely versatile, as it can accommodate articles of any size. It is a useful companion to the more stationary square frame when working stitch samples and experimental pieces. Its disadvantage, especially when working with fine fabrics and silk, is that the fabric must usually be moved as work progresses and so may be marked or otherwise damaged by the hoop. Stitches, too, may become distorted. To some extent this can be avoided by either binding the inner hoop with cotton tape, which will hold fine fabrics more firmly and prevent their slipping while being mounted (a), or covering the main fabric with another, such as muslin, and mounting them together (b). The upper fabric is cut away leaving only a protective border

around the hoop. The latter method is useful, for example, when you have to move and remount the fabric to work a large object, such as a tablecloth, section by section. It will prevent the damage of previously completed stitchery.

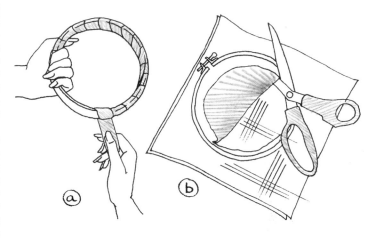

To mount fabric in a round frame. If you are using two layers of fabric—i.e. the main fabric and a backing fabric—first place them flat on a table, with their grains aligned, and tack [baste] them together through the centre in both directions (c).

Proceed as follows. Place the inner hoop on a table. Adjust the outer hoop so that it is very slightly larger than the inner one. Place the fabric on top of the inner hoop (d). Place the outer hoop over the inner one and push down firmly. Adjust the tension of the fabric by easing it through the hoops and at the same time gradually tightening the outer hoop, making sure the weave remains square (e). Do not try to pull the fabric once the outer hoop has been secured as it may tear or distort around the edge.

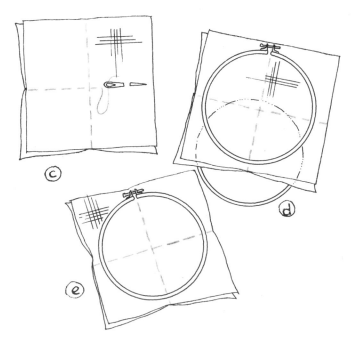

To mount fabric smaller than the hoop. If the fabric to be worked is smaller than the hoop, a secondary fabric (later removed) can be sewn around it to make it large enough for mounting. Place the piece of fabric to be embroidered onto a larger backing fabric with grains aligned. Sew the two together around the edge of the small piece, using close running stitches. Mount the fabric in the hoop as usual (a). Then either cut away the backing fabric on the wrong side (b) or work the embroidery through both layers.

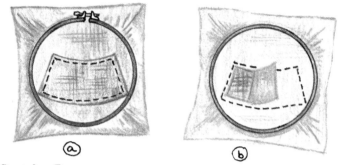

Stretcher Frames

Some materials should not be put in a round frame at all. These are nets and laces, which are easily distorted, and suedes and leathers, which easily mark. For such materials a stretcher frame is useful. Artists' stretcher frames in various sizes may be bought in art supply shops and are easily assembled. The fabric is attached with small nails or drawing pins [thumbtacks].

A useful home-made stretcher frame consists of a rectangular picture frame, or a piece of hardboard [particle

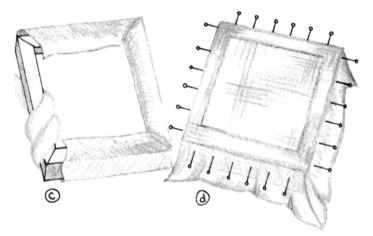

board] with a hole cut in it, which is wrapped with padding of some kind and covered with fabric (c). The embroidery fabric can then be simply laid over the frame and pinned in place through the padding (d).

Square Frames

Also known as slate frames, these are suitable for all types of embroidery and are made in several sizes. The size corresponds to the lengths of cotton webbing which are nailed to the top and bottom edges of the frame. The length of the webbing dictates the width of the fabric which may be applied. A 60 cm (24 in) frame will accommodate an embroidery with a maximum finished width of 50 cm (20 in). This allows for a 2.5 cm (1 in) turning [hem] around the work (though ideally 5 cm [2 in] or more should be allowed if it is to be mounted on a board afterwards) and a further 2.5 cm (1 in) on each side for the application and tensioning of the backing fabric and/or the

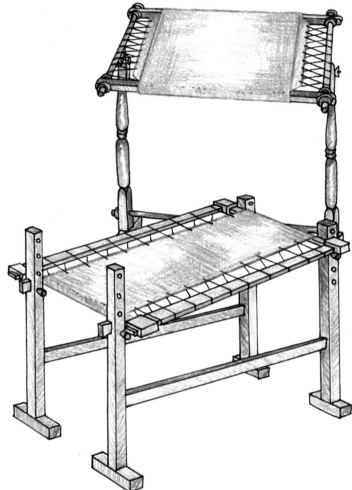

main fabric. The sides of the frame are held parallel by two bars which are fixed in place by pegs or screw fittings.

A square frame allows the whole, or at least a large part, of the work to be visible. The width may be limited to some extent by the frame size but the length is not. A long piece of fabric can be rolled around the back roller of the frame and gradually unrolled and rolled onto the front as the work proceeds.

Some square frames are made to fit onto special floor stands which allow them to pivot, so holding the fabric at the correct angle for working. If it is necessary to view the embroidery from a distance the frame can be held vertically in the stand. The height of most pivoting frames, however, is not adjustable. Another kind of frame can be adjusted to different heights. It rests on a pair of floor stands fitted with horizontal bars which can be positioned at different levels and angles by the simple use of pegs. This type of stand is extremely adaptable, as it can support any length of frame and can also be converted into a temporary table by placing a piece of board on top. A square frame need not have a special stand at all, however. It can simply be supported between two chairs or tables as long as it is stable.

It is important, though, that the frame be at a comfortable height and at the correct angle, and set up in a well-lit area. Before setting to work, arrange all necessary yarns and tools within easy reach.

Framing up is an extremely important procedure. If it is done carefully the fabric will be stretched very evenly and will remain so with perhaps only minor adjustments.

To mount a backing fabric on a square frame. If you are using a backing fabric, either for extra weight or if your embroidery is considerably smaller than the frame, you should first mount the support fabric on the frame.

Begin by preparing the backing fabric: cut it on the straight grain about 2.5–5 cm (1–2 in) larger all round than the main fabric. Take two lengths of macramé string and make a knot at both ends of each. Make a turning [hem] of approximately 1.5 cm ($\frac{5}{8}$ in) along opposite sides of the fabric, enclosing a length of string in each. Sew the turnings in place with running stitches, keeping the weave straight. Mark the centre point of the webbing on the frame with a backstitch using contrasting thread. Mark the centre point of the fabric along the top and bottom edges (those without string) with a pin (1). Fold under 1.5 cm ($\frac{5}{8}$ in) on both edges and press. Match the centres of the two folded edges to the centres of the webbing and pin them together, with fabric overlapping webbing. Using strong thread and starting at the centre, oversew [overcast] fabric and webbing together, stretching the fabric slightly while doing so (2). Fasten off thread securely. The stitches should be about

3 mm ($\frac{1}{8}$ in) apart, so as to make a very firm join that will withstand tensioning. Insert the side poles of the frame and fix them so that the fabric lies flat but not under tension.

Prepare the main fabric. Allow enough for a 5 cm (2 in) turning [hem] around the perimeter of the design. If the design is circular, always start with a square piece of fabric. Mark the centre with horizontal and vertical lines of tacking [basting]. Position it on the backing fabric with grains aligned and vertical centres matching and pin it in place (3). Sew the two fabrics together. Start from the centre on each side. Work alternating long and short straight stitches spaced at 6 mm ($\frac{1}{4}$ in) intervals around the edge of the main fabric. When the fabric is tensioned, the strain will be dispersed so that neither fabric nor 'holding' stitches will split or break.

Tension the fabric fully by first repositioning the fixing points in the side poles, holding them in place with the pegs. Then, using a large needle and string, lace the backing fabric to the sides of the frame as in the diagram (4). Pull the string up evenly on both sides until the fabric is evenly stretched like a drum. It is now ready for transferring the design.

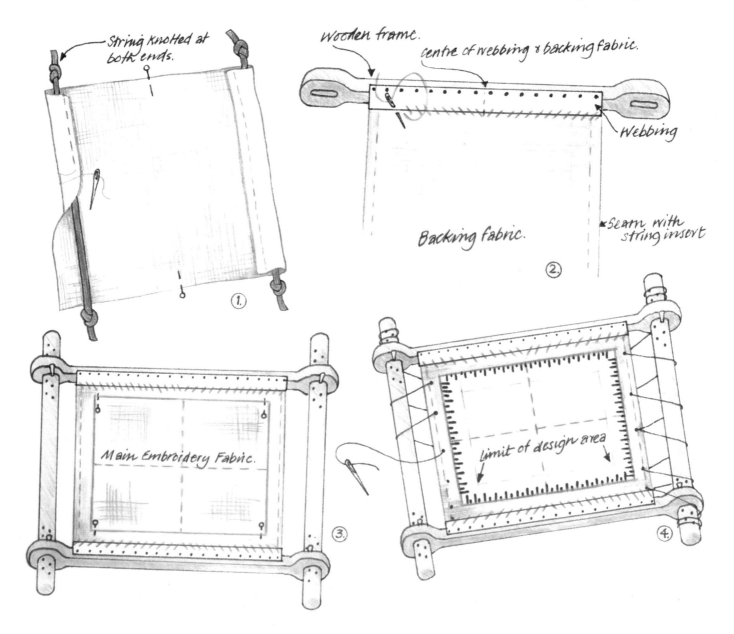

FINISHING TECHNIQUES

Embroidery worked on a square frame, or stretcher frame, should require, when completed, only a light pressing on the back. Lay the work on a soft blanket to avoid flattening the stitches. Or prop up the frame vertically, without removing the fabric, and apply the iron to the wrong side. Never press embroidery on the right side. If a round frame has been used the work may require the addition of steam, or a light spray with de-ionized water to help ease out creases or folds.

If the stitching is thick or dense you may need to block the work in order to remove creases caused by the frame. First soak the work in cold water, then lay it right side up, while still wet, on a board covered with a clean cloth, such as an old sheet. Nail it to the board, using carpet tacks or drawing pins [thumbtacks] and beginning with the corners (make sure they are square). Continue nailing all four sides, alternately, starting in the middle and pulling the fabric taut. The tacks or drawing pins [thumbtacks] should be placed at intervals of about 1.5 cm ($\frac{5}{8}$ in). Allow the work to dry thoroughly.

The techniques for making up [finishing] will depend on the function of the completed article. A hanging, for example, will require a lining and perhaps an interlining as well. These fabrics should not be heavier than the embroidery itself. They are added to protect the back of the work and help to keep the shape, as well as giving a neat finish. As much thought should be given to choosing the type and colour of the lining fabric as to choosing the main fabric. It may be sufficient to use a neutral curtain [drapery] lining material, but something more interesting, such as a patterned fabric, will add contrast and a touch of originality.

A lining should never be too tight; if it is, the edges of the work will curl under. Equally it should never be too loose or bulky, or it will be seen from the front (unless that is the intention). This is important when lining a large hanging, for example.

To Line a Hanging

Lay the work face down on a table and mark the centre from top to bottom with a row of pins. Fold the lining in half, right sides together, and lay the fold down the centre of the hanging. Working from top to bottom, join the two together with a loose lock stitch (see diagram). Smooth the lining out over the back of the hanging. Turn under the top and side edges to within 1.5 cm ($\frac{5}{8}$ in) of the outer edge of the hanging and slipstitch them together. Leave the finishing of the bottom edge until the work has been hung for a few days and all the layers of fabric have settled. Then slipstitch this edge as you did the others. The lining for a small hanging need be fixed only around the edges and not in the centre.

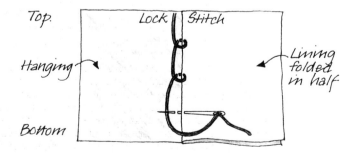

Methods of Hanging

The two simplest and safest ways of hanging the work are by means of a length of dowelling or a batten inserted through the work or through a sleeve of fabric sewn to the back of the work,

or by attaching Velcro® tape to the lining and the wall. Both methods distribute the weight of the hanging evenly along the top edge.

Hanging with dowelling or a batten. When attaching the lining, simply leave a gap at the upper side edges, wide enough to insert the dowelling. The dowelling should be slightly longer than the width of the embroidery so that a cord can be attached to either side. A second length can be inserted along the bottom edge if it requires weighting. Alternatively, lead weights—the type used for curtains [draperies]—can be sewn inside the lining.

If you wish the support to be invisible, use a batten, rather

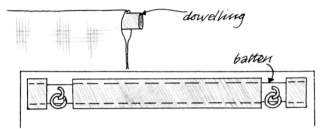

than dowelling, and attach it to the back of the work with an extra length of fabric. Cut the batten 1.5 cm ($\frac{5}{8}$ in) shorter than the width of the finished embroidery. Cut a 'sleeve' as long as the embroidery is wide and wide enough to take the batten. Make and attach it in three sections as in the diagram (above), leaving two gaps for attaching a cord or picture rings to the batten.

Hanging with Velcro®. The width of the tape used will depend on the size and weight of the embroidery. It is obtainable in 1.2–5 cm ($\frac{1}{2}$–2 in) widths. The soft side should be sewn to the back of the work with running stitches, and the hooked side nailed to a length of wood which has been nailed to the wall.

If the hanging is very heavy you must take the stitches attaching the Velcro® through to the right side; otherwise (unless there is an interlining) the work may become distorted. Choose a thread that blends into the work. (This also applies when hanging with dowelling or a batten; see above.)

To Finish a Decorative Panel

Panels may be framed, with or without glass. But before you frame a panel—or take it to a professional framer—you must mount it over a stiff backing. This keeps the fabric taut and displays the stitches to best advantage.

If the work is to be framed without a mount [matt] (see 'Double mounting'), the backing board should be 6 mm ($\frac{1}{4}$ in) larger all round than the area of the finished design to allow a margin to fit under the frame. If there will be a mount [matt] the board should be cut aproximately 3–6 mm ($\frac{1}{8}$–$\frac{1}{4}$ in) smaller all round. The bulk of the backing fabric makes up the size.

Depending on the size and weight of the embroidery, you can use either thick, white, acid-free cardboard or hardboard [particleboard]. Whichever you choose, a better finish will result if it is first covered with fabric, such as plain flannelette, to protect the work from any sharp edges.

Lay the fabric flat on a table. Lay the board on top (the rough side of hardboard [particleboard] uppermost). Paint a thin line of PVA woodworking adhesive around the edge of the board (1). Fold and stretch the fabric over onto the glue, mitring the corners, and press down firmly (2). Leave the board to dry. NEVER put glue over the front of the board or on the back of the embroidery itself.

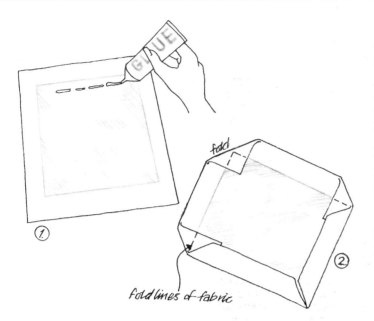

fold

fold lines of fabric

① ②

Turn the board. Draw a long length of thread from the reel, cut it off and lace from the centre to the opposite end. Do not fasten off the thread. Remove the pins from the edge.

Starting at the fastened-off corner, pull the thread firmly through each stitch so that the fabric is tightly and evenly tensioned (5). Then fasten off the thread firmly. Repeat the procedure for the other sides. Make sure that the corners sit neatly, without cutting away any fabric (6).

If the work is to be glazed as well as framed, the glass should be set away from the embroidery so as not to crush the stitches. If the panel is to remain unframed, neaten the back by attaching a lining fabric as for a hanging. Sew a cord to the back for hanging it.

Double mounting. Panels can be given a very professional finish by mounting them as described above and then covering a second, larger board with a complementary fabric, onto which the panel is sewn using a curved needle (7).

In the case of metal thread work, a thicker covering is required to act as a padding over the board. A double layer of wadding [batting] may be glued down as above, or simply taped in place until the embroidery has been stretched over it.

Lacing the work to the board. Lay the embroidery face down on a clean surface with the covered board positioned on top (3). Pin the embroidery to the cloth of the board around the edges. Lift the panel carefully and check from the front that the work is square.

Thread a needle with strong button thread, without cutting it off the reel. Starting at the centre of one long side, work herringbone stitch across the board, lacing two sides of the embroidery together (4). When you reach the end, fasten off the thread firmly.

③ ④ ⑤ ⑥

CARE OF EMBROIDERY

Never hang embroidery in direct sunlight or near bright spotlights. Heat and light cause colours to fade and fabrics and threads to weaken and age quickly. Try to avoid placing a hanging above heating appliances and radiators. The rising dry, hot air and dust will make the work brittle and dirty.

Frequent washing and ironing should be avoided if at all possible. Embroidered household linen and furnishings can be washed gently by hand in a mild liquid detergent and luke-warm water if dyes are fast. They should be dried flat, right side uppermost, on a smooth surface. If the weave is laid square and smooth and left until dry, little or no ironing at all will be required, resulting in the embroidery looking fresh and crisp.

If dyes are not colour-fast then the embroidery must be dry cleaned. Very fine work and mounted panels should be taken to a specialist cleaner. If embroidery must be stored for any length of time it should always be cleaned first and packed in white acid-free tissue. Keep it in a dark, dry place and check it frequently for moths. If a piece is too large to be stored flat it should be rolled with the right side out—so as not to crush the embroidery—around a cardboard tube, then wrapped in layers of tissue and finally in a clean cover-cloth. Never store it in polythene or plastic bags, as the static electricity created attracts dust, and the textile is not allowed to 'breathe'.

If in doubt about cleaning or storage seek the advice of the conservation department of your local museum.

STITCH GLOSSARY

The following stitch glossary includes only a small selection of the hundreds devised over the centuries. Many traditional stitches, such as *long and short stitch* and *cross stitch*, still remain favourites, whereas others have been forgotten. Several stitches are known by more than one name, and even these may differ from country to country. For instance, *cretan stitch*, worked as a line stitch, is also called *long-armed feather stitch* or *spine stitch*, and *chained feather stitch* may also be called *long-armed zig-zag chain*.

The name of a stitch, however, is unimportant if it provides the required effect, and the way of working it will differ from person to person depending on individual skill and manual dexterity. Learning to work a stitch in the 'correct' manner is satisfying and brings confidence, but exciting discoveries and new variations can emerge from so-called 'mistakes'. An individual style of working gives the embroidery a fresh, innovative appearance. Whether the style is neat and formal or free and apparently haphazard, the work will have a timeless quality. This may be achieved unconsciously, but is something to be aimed at.

RUNNING STITCH

This is one of the oldest and simplest of stitches. It is used for making outlines and creating simple line effects, and also as a foundation for overcast stitch. The needle is passed regularly over and under the fabric. If worked without a frame, several stitches can be made at a time.

RUNNING STITCH VARIATIONS

(a) In whipped running stitch a second thread is laced through the stitches, without passing through the fabric. To avoid splitting the thread, use the blunt end of the needle, or a tapestry needle.

(b) In this variation two threads are laced through the stitches, without being drawn tightly.
(c) Threading through rows is another alternative.
(d) Double running stitch, shown here, is also known as Holbein stitch; the second row of running stitches is worked into the same holes made by the first.

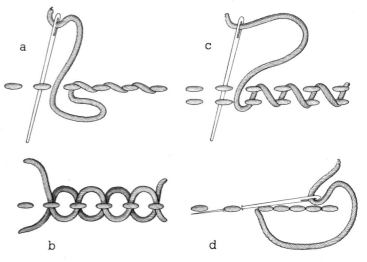

BACK STITCH

Back stitch is usually worked in small, neat, even stitches and resembles machine stitching in appearance. In modern free embroidery, however, the stitches may vary in length and be worked quite haphazardly. First make a stitch backwards, bringing the needle out some way in front of the starting point. Then make another stitch backwards to meet the beginning of the last stitch, and so on (a). This is one of the basic stitches used to work the endless varieties of patterns found in black work. Because the stitch can turn corners neatly, it is ideally suited to the crisp and sometimes complex outlines of these patterns. Each back stitch is worked over a specific number of threads, so as to produce identical motifs (b). In the example shown (c) back stitch is used for the outlines and cross stitches as fillings. The pattern can appear open or solid by subtracting or adding back stitches to the basic unit shape.

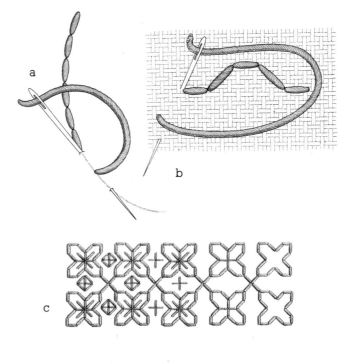

PEKINESE STITCH

This is a very pretty stitch used widely in Chinese embroidery, mainly as a filling. Worked finely and close together it resembles rows of little French knots. It can also be worked in metal threads. A base row of even back stitches is worked first, through which a second thread is looped, as shown. Use the blunt end of the needle or a tapestry needle for the second thread, to avoid catching the back stitches and previous loops.

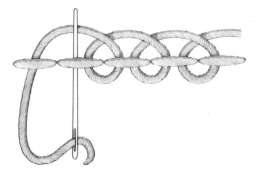

STEM STITCH

Keeping the thread on the same side of the needle throughout, make regular and even stitches, bringing the needle out to the left, halfway along the previous stitch. The stitches overlap each other in a fine, straight line used for outlines, lines and fillings.

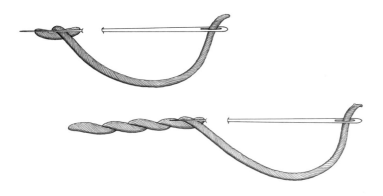

WHIPPED STEM STITCH

Work a row of stem stitch. Then pass a second thread under two stitches where they overlap—but not into the fabric. Pass over the stitches, then under again, working in the opposite direction to that of the stem stitch. Use the blunt end of the needle or a tapestry needle to avoid splitting the stem stitches.

PORTUGUESE KNOTTED STEM STITCH

This stitch looks best when worked with a single thread such as coton à broder, pearl cotton or tapestry wool. The knobbly effect created by whipping the stem stitches together adds texture to a design. Begin as for ordinary stem stitch but, before proceeding to the next stitch, pass the blunt end of the needle under the first stitch twice without piercing the fabric. Make the next stem stitch and whip it and the top of the previous stitch together twice, and so on.

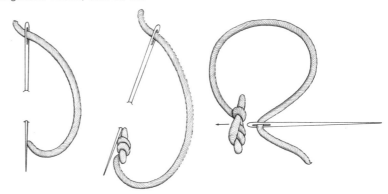

FRENCH KNOTS

To make a French knot, bring the thread up at the desired place, wrap the thread once around the point of the needle and re-insert the needle. Hold down the thread firmly with the thumb and pull the needle through smoothly and swiftly. The knots should be kept neat and precise and look like little round beads. To increase the size of the knots, use a thicker thread or more strands of the same thread.

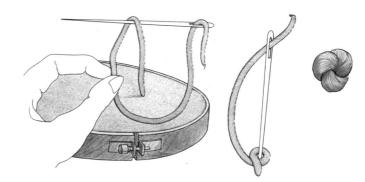

BULLION KNOTS

These require some practice in order to keep the twists of the knot even. The number of twists can vary depending on the yarn and the desired size of the knot. The more twists made, the greater the skill required. Practise first with only three or four twists and a single thread such as coton à broder. Bring the needle up and make a back stitch, bringing the needle up again at the starting point, but not pulling it through yet. Push the needle through as far as the eye, then wrap the thread around the point the desired number of times. Hold down the twisted thread, which should be coiled firmly, but not tightly, to enable the needle to pass through smoothly with least disturbance to the twists. Quickly take the needle down where it was inserted before and pull the thread firmly.

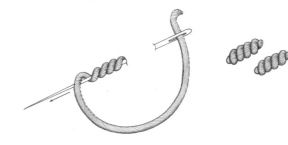

19

SPLIT STITCH

This is worked in somewhat the same way as stem stitch, but instead of coming up to one side of the previous stitch, the needle pierces the thread as it comes up through the fabric. The resulting smooth, flat surface makes this stitch ideal as a filling, particularly in figurative designs, where it is often used to embroider heads and hands.

DETACHED CHAIN STITCH OR LAZY DAISY STITCH

This is worked in the same way as chain stitch, except that each loop is secured individually with a small straight stitch. Single free-standing loops can be made by working the small straight stitch over the point where the needle enters the fabric, instead of over the loop.

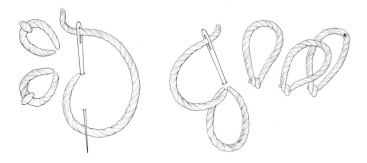

CHAIN STITCH

This is one of the most often-used embroidery stitches both in its simple form and in its countless variations. Basic chain stitch can be used for lines, for outlines or as a filling. Bring the needle through and insert it again into the same hole, so forming a loop. Holding the loop down with the thumb, bring the needle up again through the loop, a short distance away from the starting point, and pull the thread through. Insert the needle into the same hole, still inside the loop, and make a second loop. Repeat, forming a row of loops, each one securing the previous one.

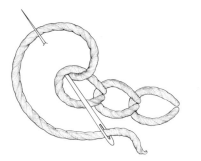

OPEN CHAIN STITCH

This is often seen in Indian and West Turkestan embroideries worked in wide bands as borders or to fill motifs. Bring the needle out at the left and insert it a short distance to the right; then take it diagonally to the left, inside the loop, and reinsert it to the right, still inside the loop. The result is a series of widened loops.

WHIPPED CHAIN STITCH

Work a row of basic chain stitch. Then, using a blunt needle and a second thread, which can be of a contrasting colour, come up at the beginning of the row and pass the needle under each chain loop from right to left. This binds the loops, forming a slightly raised line which is good for marking precise outlines.

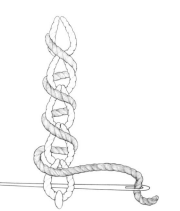

CABLE CHAIN STITCH

This looks like a row of alternating loops and straight stitches. Work the first stitch as for basic chain, but after bringing the needle up to begin the next loop, twist the thread once around it; then insert the needle *outside* the first loop and bring it up as shown inside the new loop; draw the stitch flat. As with basic chain stitch, this can also be worked in a zig-zag formation.

TWISTED CHAIN STITCH

This gives a more textured effect than ordinary chain stitch. Instead of inserting the needle into the same hole inside each loop, bring it over the loop and insert it slightly to the left, outside the new loop. Then bring the needle up through this loop, and repeat, producing a row of twisted loops. The stitches should be worked close together for the maximum effect.

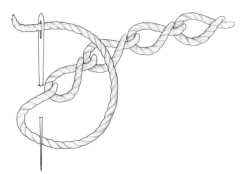

ROSETTE CHAIN STITCH

This is a very decorative stitch and appears more complicated than it is. The stitches are worked side by side, from right to left. Begin as if making a twisted chain stitch. After bringing the needle up at the bottom of the loop, pass it under the top of the loop, and then take it across to the left of the first chain at the position for the next stitch. Work another twisted chain stitch, passing the needle under the thread at the top as before. Keep the thread slightly loose. Each twisted chain stitch is then linked to the rest along the top of the row.

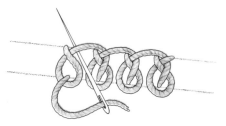

RAISED CHAIN BAND

First make a foundation row of parallel, horizontal straight stitches. Then work the chain stitch from top to bottom over the bars. Bring the needle up through the fabric at the top centre of the first bar and pass it over and under the bar to the left (not through the fabric). Holding the stitch in place, take the needle to the right of it and slip it under the bar and over the loop formed. Without pulling the thread very taut, bring the needle over and under the next bar to begin the next stitch. The bars and chains can be worked in different colours and threads.

CORAL STITCH

This is known by several names including bead stitch and snail trail. It is a simple, knotted line stitch, which can be arranged as a filling. The knots, worked in a similar manner to a twisted chain stitch, punctuate the straight thread at intervals.

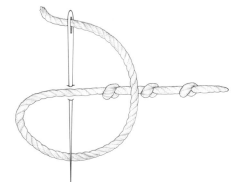

CROSS STITCH

One of the oldest and most versatile of all embroidery stitches, cross stitch is found in the traditional work of the Scandinavian countries and central and eastern Europe, down to the Greek Islands and Turkey. It is most easily worked on evenweave fabric, on which the warp and weft threads can be counted for each stitch, producing stitches of identical size. It can be worked in two ways. In one method, shown at right, an individual cross is completed before the next is begun. In the other, a line of diagonal stitches is made in one direction and is then crossed by another line of diagonal stitches worked in the opposite direction. This method is preferable for lines or blocks of cross stitch, in which it is important that all top and bottom stitches slant in the same direction. On fine fabrics, on which threads cannot be counted, it is possible to work precise cross stitches by first tacking [basting] evenweave canvas over the framed fabric. Work the stitch over the canvas as shown at left. Then dampen the work and pull out the canvas thread by thread.

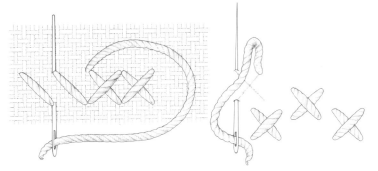

ST. GEORGE CROSS STITCH

This is most often used on evenweave fabric, on which the threads can be counted to keep the horizontal and vertical stitches even.

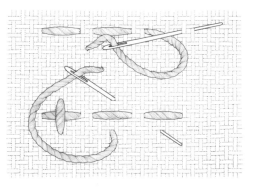

LONG-ARMED CROSS STITCH OR LONG-LEGGED CROSS STITCH

This stitch is most easily mastered by practising on an even-weave fabric. Bring the needle up and count eight threads to the right and four up from the starting point. Take the needle down at this point, forming a long diagonal stitch. Cross this stitch from the bottom right to the top left over a square of four threads. Bring the needle up four threads from the starting point so that it is ready to make the next diagonal stitch. The first long diagonal dictates the shape of the stitch and gives it its name.

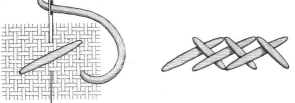

HERRINGBONE STITCH

This very adaptable stitch lends itself to many variations. The stitches can be set wide apart (a) or close together and can be threaded and interlaced, as in example (b), forming different patterns. It is the basic stitch used for shadow work, in which it is worked close together (c) on the underside of transparent fabric. This produces, on the right side, two rows of small back stitches, which give the stitch—worked in this way—the name double back stitch.

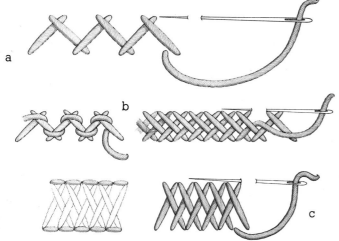

CHEVRON STITCH

This stitch can be worked on evenweave fabric, or it can be made between two parallel lines of tacking [basting] so that the diagonal stitches are kept even. Work in a similar way to herringbone stitch but do not cross the diagonal stitches. Instead, bring the needle up a short distance behind the diagonal, insert it the same distance in front, then bring it out at the end of the diagonal to begin the next stitch.

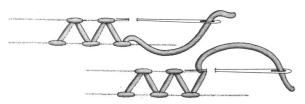

VANDYKE STITCH

This is worked from top to bottom, the first stitch providing the anchor for the subsequent central loops. The needle passes through the fabric at each side, but not at the centre—except on the first stitch. If the stitches are pulled too tightly the plaited [braided] effect will be distorted.

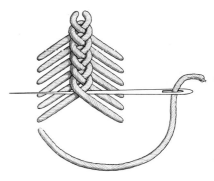

STRAIGHT STITCH

This stitch is also known as single satin stitch. It is widely used in modern free embroidery. It is useful for laying down large areas of colour quickly and for creating direction in a design. It can be placed at random over the fabric or at regular, spaced intervals as a filling.

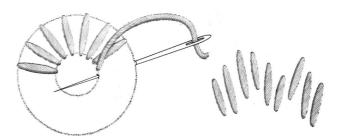

LONG AND SHORT STITCH

This stitch is used to create beautiful, subtle effects of shading and can be used to fill large, irregular areas where satin stitches would become too long and untidy. Practice is required in order to achieve the smooth transition from one line of stitches to the next. First work a row of split stitch around the outline of the shape to be filled. Start the first row by bringing the needle up inside the shape and taking it down just outside the line of split stitches. Follow the outline closely, alternating long and short stitches and placing each stitch close beside its neighbour. Work the second and subsequent rows of stitches of equal length in brick fashion to fill in the gaps between the upper stitches. Work outwards from the centre.

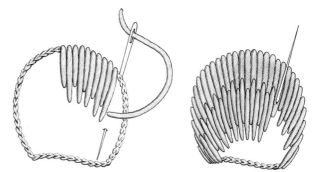

OVERCAST STITCH

This stitch resembles a fine cord and is most often used in white work for stems and outlines. It can look as neat on the back as on the front of the work. The small, close stitches are raised slightly by first laying down a row of running stitches or by working them over one or more laid threads.

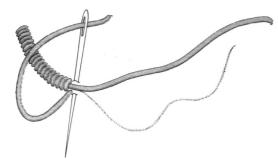

SATIN STITCH

This stitch is the main stitch used for the geometric patterns of Hardanger embroidery and is also one of the basic stitches for pulled fabric work, where, by varying the tension, one can create different patterns on the evenweave fabric. In free embroidery it is used for fillings and shaded effects. The stitches, best worked on a frame, can be of varying lengths but must lie flat and even, giving a beautiful smooth finish with precise outlines. Though simple in structure it is a difficult stitch to work well, but the finished effect is well worth the trouble.

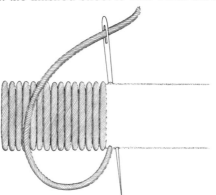

RAISED OR PADDED SATIN STITCH

By first laying a foundation or padding of different types of stitches, and then covering them entirely with satin stitch worked in the usual way, one can produce a slightly raised effect, which adds depth and interest to otherwise flat work.
(a) The motif is first outlined with split stitch or back stitch and the satin stitches are worked over and close to this outline. This technique gives more definition to the edge of the shape.

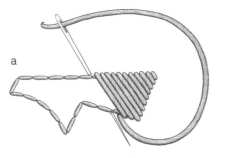

(b) The motif is first filled with tiny seeding stitches or running stitch. These can be worked thicker on one side of the shape than on the other, so that once covered by the satin stitches they will produce an effect of graduated relief.

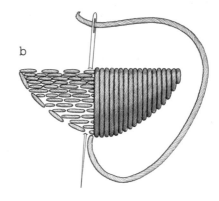

(c) Satin stitch is first worked across the entire motif with the threads lying in one direction. A second layer of satin stitch, slanting in the opposite direction, is then worked over the first. Several layers of stitches can be worked in this way until quite a high relief is obtained, but care must be taken not to distort the outline.

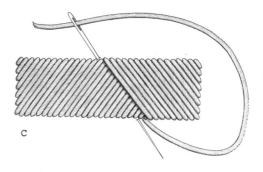

ROUMANIAN STITCH

Begin by laying down a straight stitch from left to right across the desired width of the stitch. Then bring the needle up a third of the way from the end, just above the thread, and make an oblique stitch across it to hold it in place. Bring the needle up again just beside the starting point and repeat. Keep the stitches close together. A pattern will be formed by the oblique couching stitches.

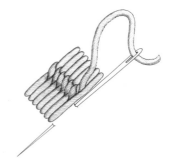

FISHBONE STITCH

This filling stitch is useful for shaped motifs or wide bands.
(a) Begin by making a small straight stitch at the centre top of the motif. Then work sloping stitches alternately to the right and left, taking the needle down just below the end of the previous stitch.
(b) For open fishbone stitch work the stitches wider apart.

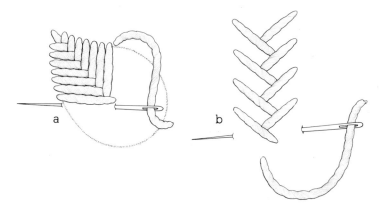

FLAT STITCH

Used to fill a shape, this stitch has the appearance of two blocks of satin stitch, worked side by side, each encroaching on the other in the centre. As a guide for working the stitch, two lines can be drawn inside the shape as shown. The stitch can begin from either the left or right side and can be worked either from inner line to edge (a) or from edge to inner line (b).

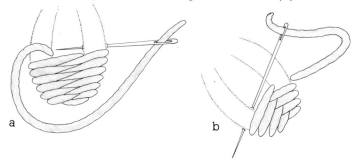

CRETAN STITCH

This decorative filling stitch can be adapted to fit almost any size and shape of motif. The stitches can be placed close together as in (a) or apart as in (b), and the loops can be horizontal or sloped. In example (c) the loops have become straight diagonal stitches.

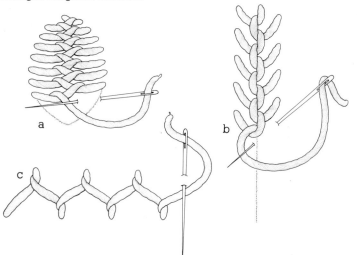

FLY STITCH

This is worked in a similar way to chain stitch except that the loop is open at the top and forms a 'Y' when tied down with the straight stitch. The stitch can be worked singly (a) or in rows (b), one under the other.

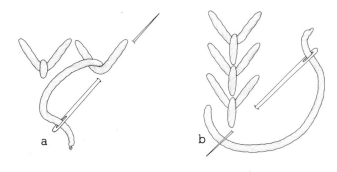

FEATHER STITCH

This stitch is made up of a series of loops, placed to the right and to the left, each one holding the previous loop in place. It is generally worked in a line from top to bottom and is often used on smocks for surface embroidery and as a smocking stitch.

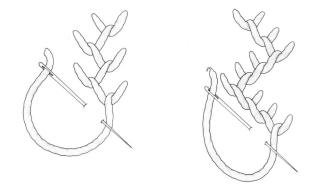

CHAINED FEATHER STITCH

Work this stitch between two parallel lines. Begin on either the left or right side and move diagonally towards the opposite side. Make a slanting chain stitch, tying it down with a longer straight stitch than usual. Then make a second chain stitch in the other direction and so on. The tying stitches must form a regular zig-zag pattern.

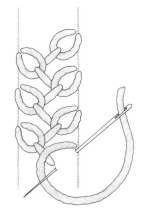

BLANKET STITCH

Also called buttonhole stitch, this is formed by taking a straight stitch to one side of the previous one, with the thread under the needle point, so forming a loop when the stitch is pulled up. The straight stitches can be spaced slightly apart (a) or close together (b), of equal length or of varying lengths and grouped to form different patterns (c) and (d). If worked close together the stitch can be used as a filling or as an edging for cut work.

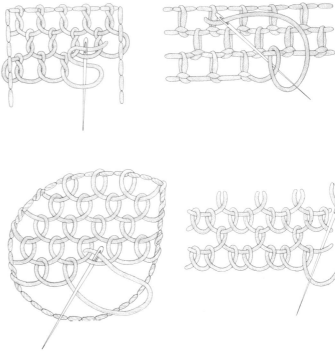

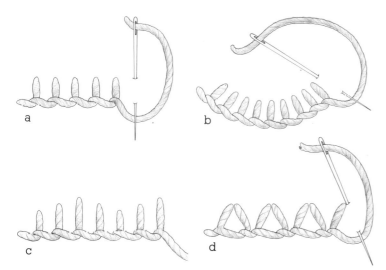

DETACHED BUTTONHOLE LACE STITCH FILLING

This is essentially blanket—or buttonhole—stitch worked on itself and detached from the ground fabric except at the edges. Like other lace fillings, it can be worked around a circle to the centre or from one side of a shape to the other.
1. Outline the design shape with a single thread couched down to the fabric.
2. From left to right, work the first row of buttonhole loops over this outline, passing the needle under the couched thread at the end of the row.
3. Take the needle straight back to the left side, and pass it under the couched thread.
4. Work another row of loops, this time taking the needle under the previous loops and the straight thread at the same time.
5. Continue in this way, working rows of loops over the straight threads. The pattern of loops can be varied, as shown, and can also be worked without an outline.

A back stitch can be used to anchor the thread, but if the fabric is to be cut away under the lace fillings, first work the outlines in running stitch, covered by close buttonholing. Then cut away the fabric close to the buttonhole stitch before working the lace filling.

The stitch can be worked on a paper foundation and then used as desired.
1. Draw the outline of the motif on firm tracing paper.
2. Couch a single, continuous thread to the paper around the outline. Use the same thread as will be used for the filling.
3. Work the filling. Do not take the needle through the paper but attach each row of stitches to the couched thread.
4. After filling the shape, darn in any loose ends invisibly.
5. Turn over the paper and cut the stitches holding the couched outline thread. The filled shape will then come away from the paper. It can be applied to fabric or joined with other motifs to form a needlepoint lace.

Filling Stitches

Those fillings that are worked somewhat independently of the ground fabric—i.e. laid threads held only at intervals by tiny stitches—are usually embroidered on a closely woven material such as a plain weave cotton or silk, or—following the 17th-century tradition of crewel work—on a linen-cotton twill weave mixture. Fabric used for crewel work should be of furnishing weight in order to give enough support to the crewel wools. Laid fillings are generally worked within well-defined areas.

SEEDING

This is one of the simplest filling stitches. An area of design can be filled quickly and delicately with small straight stitches of equal length placed at random.

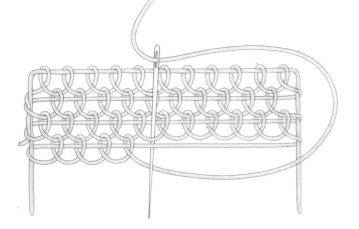

CLOUD FILLING STITCH

Make a foundation of small, regularly spaced, vertical stitches as shown. With a second thread, which is fastened to the fabric only at the ends of rows, weave in and out of the vertical stitches encompassing two rows at a time. Use the blunt end of the needle or a tapestry needle so as not to pierce the fabric or previous stitches.

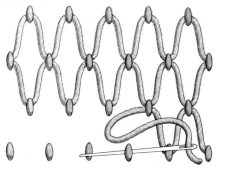

SPIDER'S WEB FILLING

Use a circle as a guide and begin by working a fly stitch, the ends of which touch the circle's circumference. Then work two straight stitches, one on each side of the fly stitch, so dividing the circle evenly into five sections. Starting at the centre, to the left of one straight stitch, weave over and under, round and round, until the circle is filled, or only half filled, as required.

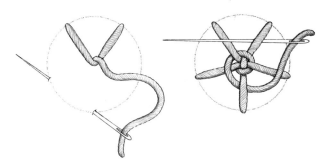

ERMINE FILLING

Begin by making a straight, vertical stitch, then cross it with an elongated cross stitch which is slightly shorter than the straight stitch. Stitches are usually placed in a spaced, brick pattern, so forming a light filling; or they can be worked close together in rows to give a more dense effect.

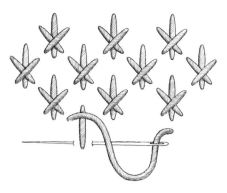

STAR FILLING STITCH

This can be used in the same way as ermine stitch or as a single star. Make a St. George cross and cover this with a diagonal cross stitch. Finally, work a tiny central cross over the whole. Different colours can be used for each cross.

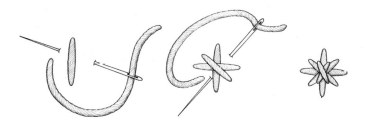

SHEAF FILLING STITCH

Begin with three vertical straight stitches, placed close together. Bring the needle up halfway down, beneath the central stitch and slide it to the left of the group. Wrap the straight stitches together twice and take the needle down to the right, near to where it emerged.

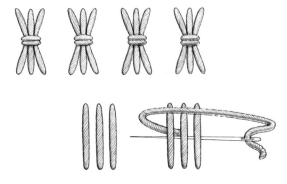

HONEYCOMB FILLING STITCH

First lay horizontal rows of parallel, spaced threads. Over these lay diagonal threads. Finally, cross these with diagonal threads laid in the other direction, weaving in and out of the previously laid rows as in the diagram. This filling is especially suitable for metal thread work, as most of the thread remains on the surface of the fabric.

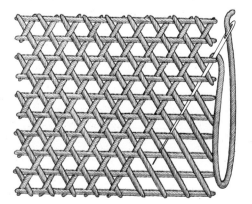

COUCHED FILLINGS OR JACOBEAN COUCHING

There are endless variations of couched fillings, and there is scope for inventing new ones. The design area is filled with a network of laid parallel, spaced threads, which are then held down at intervals with decorative stitching.

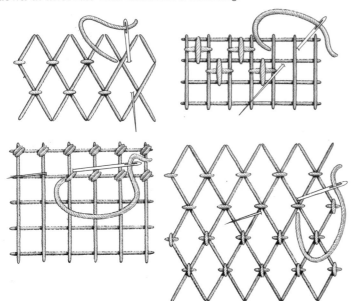

SATIN STITCH BLOCKS

Work a foundation of laid, parallel, spaced threads. Starting from one corner and working diagonally across the area, lay down blocks of satin stitch over pairs of laid threads in a chequer-board pattern. Use a tapestry needle for this work. Tiny stitches may be taken into the ground fabric at intervals to avoid distorting the pattern.

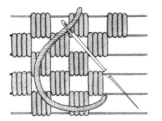

LAID WORK

Laid work is used as a solid filling for areas too large for satin stitch. The thread does not cover the underside of the motif, as in satin stitch, but is anchored to the fabric at each side of the motif. Lay the threads as shown, in two stages, placing them close together. When the area is covered, the threads are tied down with any suitable surface stitchery. On the example shown, diagonal threads have been laid across the surface and couched to the fabric with St. George's cross stitches.

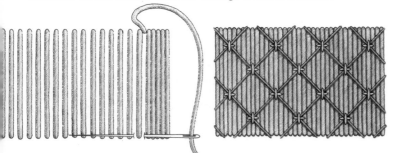

COUCHED WORK

Couched work is most often associated with metal thread embroidery, but other threads can be couched and used as fillings on their own, or in conjunction with metal threads. For basic couching, lay a thread on the fabric and tie it down with tiny stitches made at regular intervals along its length. Normally the laid thread is thicker than the one used for stitching.

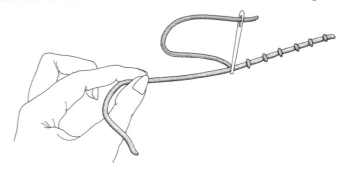

BOKHARA COUCHING OR SELF-COUCHING

In this technique the laid thread and the thread used for couching are the same. Bring the needle up and lay down a long line of thread, leaving it slightly loose. Bring the needle out back along the laid thread and make a tiny stitch at right angles across it. Proceed down the thread in this way, securing it at regular intervals. When used as a filling, the tiny couching stitches may be arranged to form various patterns.

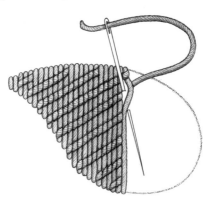

ROUMANIAN COUCHING OR FIGURE STITCH

This is worked in a similar manner to Bokhara couching except that a single, longer tying stitch is worked at an angle across the laid thread. When used as a filling, the closely worked stitches produce a diagonal ribbed effect. This stitch is useful for laying down large areas of bold colour quickly.

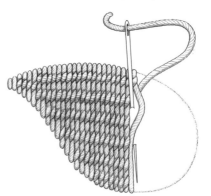

Pulled fabric work

In pulled fabric work the ground fabric is distorted by pulling the embroidery stitches tightly, so forming patterns of spaces and holes. The stitches look most effective when worked in a thread matching the colour of the fabric. Traditionally, this was white or beige, but other colours are also suitable. The stitches completely change the look of the material, and indeed become an integral part of it, rather than remaining as surface decoration. Plain, evenweave materials are best for this technique; they can range from fine linens or cottons to coarser furnishing fabrics, linen scrim and soft canvas. The weave should be slightly open to allow for ease of working and to produce the best effects. The more open the weave, the lacier the end result will be. The thread should be strong enough to withstand the strain of constant pulling, and be of comparable thickness to that of the ground fabric. This technique is best worked in a frame with the fabric under tension. This makes it possible to count the threads more easily and also helps in maintaining the correct tension while stitching. By intentionally varying the tension one can produce different effects with the same stitch. Many of the stitches shown can be used without tension for basic counted thread embroidery. For some modern pulled fabric work the fabric threads are not counted and the stitches are worked asymmetrically.

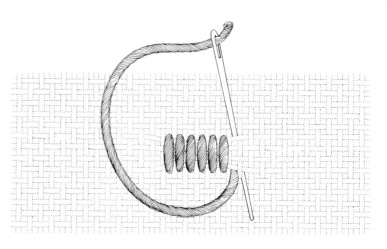

Use a tapestry needle to avoid splitting the threads. Begin and end by darning the thread invisibly into the fabric or through stitches already worked.

SATIN STITCH FILLINGS

Some of the simplest effects are created by using blocks and rows of satin stitch worked vertically, horizontally or diagonally over various numbers of threads. The stitches are pulled up with the appropriate amount of tension to produce the desired effect. (a) Rows of horizontal satin stitch; (b) rows of vertical satin stitch; (c and d) blocks of diagonal satin stitch.

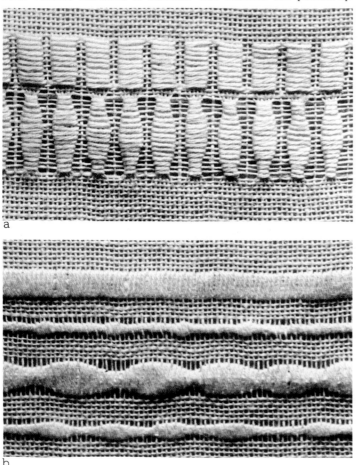

a

b

c

d

CHESSBOARD FILLING

Work a block of three horizontal rows of ten satin stitches over three threads of fabric at the upper left-hand corner of the area. Then work two blocks of three vertical rows, one below the first block and one to the right of it. Continue in this way, making alternating horizontal and vertical blocks.

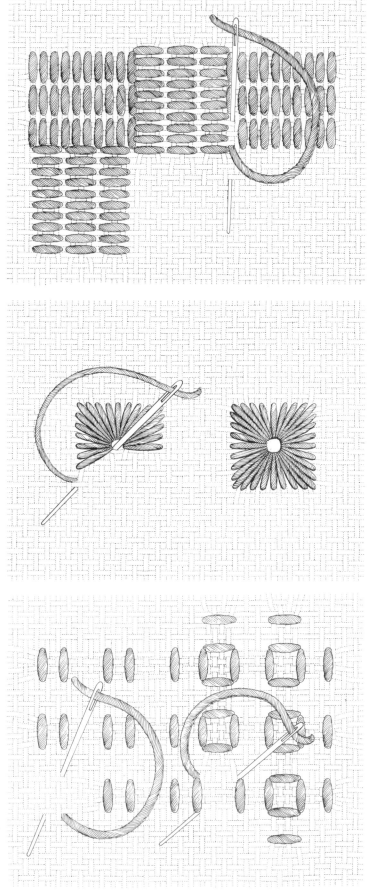

SQUARE EYELET

When forming eyelets always bring the needle up on the outer edge and down through the centre, as this makes the central hole larger. Begin in the middle of one side with a straight stitch, and work round over each thread until the shape is filled. The diagrams show an eyelet worked over eight threads.

COBBLER FILLING

This is a spaced satin stitch filling. Begin with vertical stitches; then join these with horizontal stitches to form squares as shown. Work each stitch over four threads, leaving two horizontal and two vertical threads between stitches.

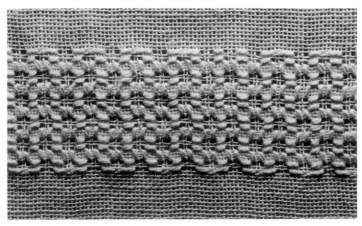

WAVE STITCH

Bring the needle up and insert it two threads to the right and four threads up; bring it out again four threads to the left. Insert it at the starting point, bring it out four threads to the left and continue in this way to the end. Turn the fabric round and work a second row to form diamond shapes. These sloping stitches will become straight when tensioned.

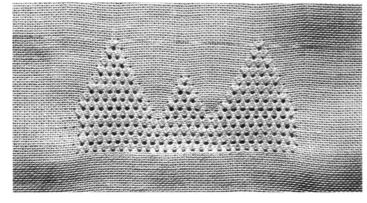

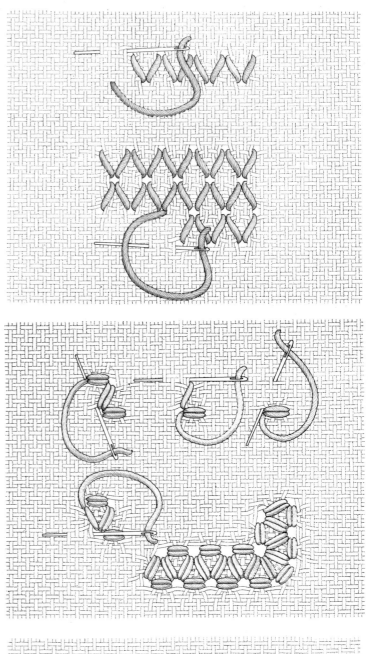

THREE-SIDED STITCH

This is useful either as a line stitch for borders or as a filling. It is made up of double back stitches worked in triangles over four threads. Working from right to left, begin at the base of the triangle with two back stitches. Then continue, following the diagram.

WAFFLE STITCH

This is shown worked over a basic square of three threads, and is made up of rows of straight vertical stitches which become slanted when tensioned. After the first row is complete, work the top of the following row into the same holes made at the bottom of the previous row.

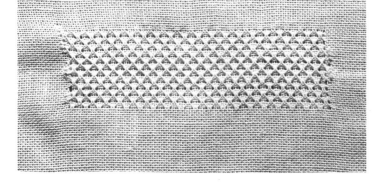

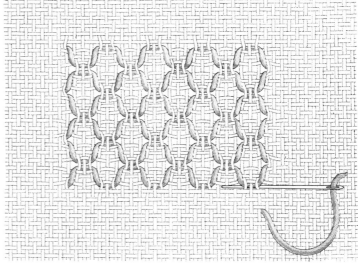

SINGLE FAGGOT STITCH

The stitches are worked in diagonal rows over a basic square of four threads. Work the first row diagonally from top to bottom, making a series of back stitches at right angles. To turn, make the last vertical a back stitch, then make another vertical stitch below this, bringing the needle up diagonally to the right. Work upwards into the same holes as upper row.

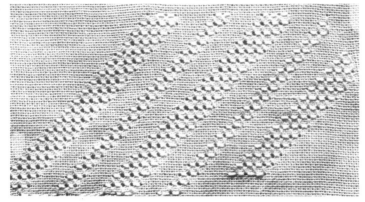

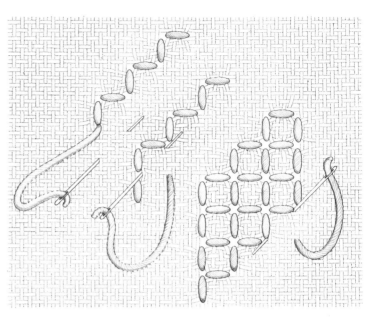

HONEYCOMB FILLING STITCH

Work from top to bottom, making alternate horizontal and vertical stitches over four threads to the right and to the left. Each vertical stitch must be a back stitch, so that the needle will be in the correct position for the horizontal stitch. When used for pulled work the stitch produces diamond shapes.

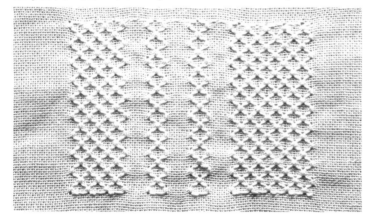

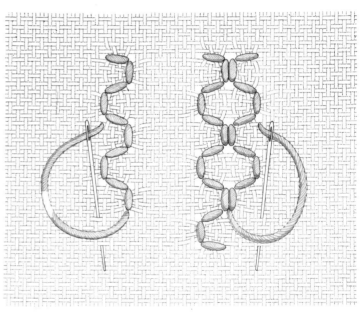

RINGED BACK STITCH

This stitch is worked from right to left. When the first row of half circles is formed, turn the fabric round to complete the rings. A single or double back stitch over two or three threads may be used, depending on the weight of fabric.

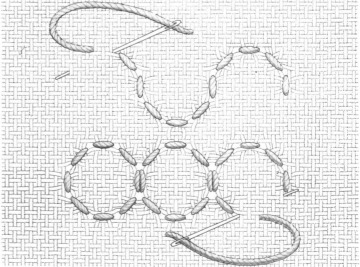

Drawn thread work

This involves carefully cutting and removing threads from an evenweave ground fabric and then working embroidery over the remaining threads. The ends of the cut threads are either darned in invisibly or held down with tiny back stitches on the wrong side. It is most often used for borders, a number of horizontal threads being removed and the remaining loose vertical threads grouped together in different patterns.

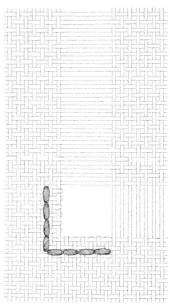

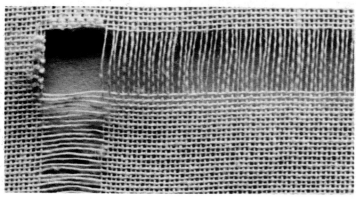

HEMSTITCH

This can be worked simply to group threads together, or as a finish to a hem, in which case it is worked from the wrong side, from left to right as shown in (a1) and (a2). It may also be worked from right to left, on the right side (b) and along both edges, in which case it is called ladder hemstitch (c).

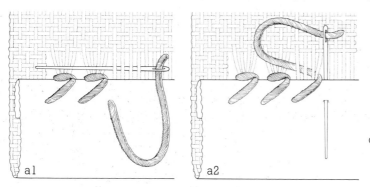

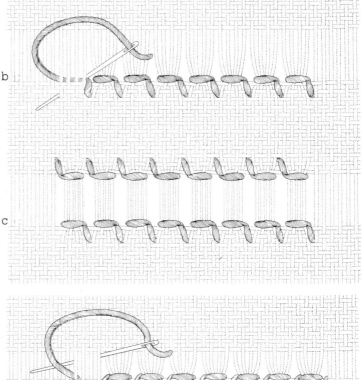

DOUBLE OR ITALIAN HEMSTITCH

Withdraw four horizontal threads of ground fabric, leave four threads and withdraw a further four threads. Work from right to left over the remaining central threads with a series of back stitches grouping threads along the top and bottom alternately.

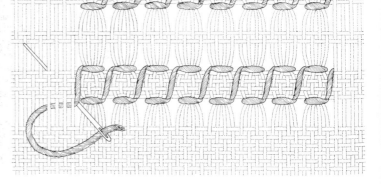

INTERLACED HEMSTITCH

Withdraw enough threads to make a deep border and work ladder hemstitch first, creating an even number of thread groups. Fasten a long thread at the right hand side and, using a tapestry needle, pass to the left and under the second group of threads, then back to the right and under the first group, so crossing the groups. Continue in this way until all the groups are crossed in pairs.

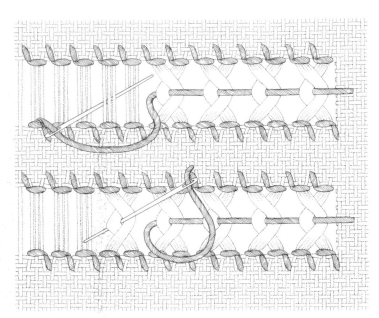

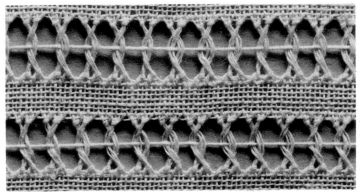

NEEDLEWEAVE WHEEL

When threads are drawn out around all four sides of the ground fabric to make a border, a hole will result at each corner. This can either be left empty or filled as in the diagram. Extra diagonal stitches are required to cross the horizontal and vertical interlacing threads at the corners, in order to provide eight spokes around which to weave the wheel.

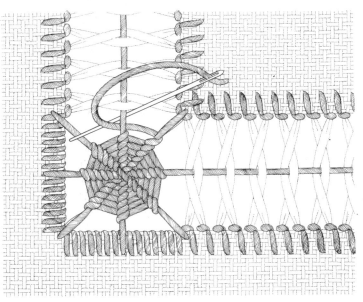

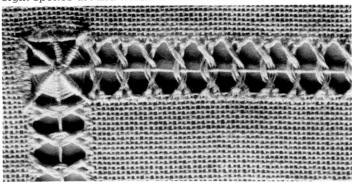

SIMPLE NEEDLEWEAVING

It is not necessary to work hemstitch first if weaving is used to group the threads. Work from top to bottom and vice versa alternately, weaving under and over two threads at a time in a figure-of-eight to form solid groups of four threads each (a). You can also increase the number of threads in each block, binding in different patterns (b), or use different-coloured threads.

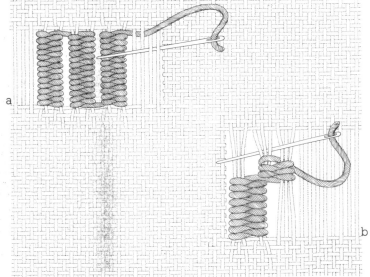

DESIGN

Most people quake in their boots at the very suggestion of creating their own designs. The first reaction is often, 'Oh, but I can't draw', implying that they cannot even begin.

Designing is a conscious action, one requiring a great deal of thought, but not necessarily the ability to put pencil to paper. Many people are technically extremely proficient at embroidery. Ask them to work a stitch or follow someone else's design and they will do it correctly and beautifully. On this level embroidery is a peaceful, comfortable activity, demanding little and offering the satisfaction of producing a piece of work admired for its execution. Those who are brave enough to attempt their own original design are rewarded with the additional satisfaction of expressing their own ideas and a greater awareness of their ability and the possibilities of their craft. It is a stretching, self-teaching process, and, like all education, involves doing things we dislike as well as those we enjoy. You may consider your first attempt a dismal failure, but you will have learnt something from it that may make the second a success.

The projects in this book will help you to increase your knowledge of the craft, which is essential before you embark on design. They will help you to develop a certain level of skill in the use of fabrics, threads and stitchery. You will find that each stitch has its own character, which varies when worked on different fabrics and with different yarns, or if the size or tension is varied. By experimenting you will discover how the characteristics of a certain fabric will influence the choice of yarns, and in time you will be able, almost instinctively, to choose the right threads for each different type of fabric, so that each complements the other (see examples 1 and 2). This is the first step in successful designing. The next will involve asking yourself some simple questions. First: What is the function of the embroidered object? Where and how will it be used? This will impose limitations on the choice of suitable fabrics and techniques. Next: How will it relate to other objects around it? For example, consider the colour scheme of the room in which it will be used, or the dress it will adorn. Should the embroidery harmonize with its surroundings, contrast with them or dominate them? What shape and size will it be? All these questions will take time and thought to answer, but the answers will—almost without your realizing it—help the design process.

Design is a very personal form of expression, which is why it is not easy to achieve. Its success depends on a knowledge not only of one's craft but also of oneself, and this is why asking questions is so important. What colours, shapes, textures do I like and why? Which do I dislike and why? Awareness of your own tastes will help you to create work imbued with your own personality, unique and easily distinguished from the work of others.

LEARNING FROM THE PAST
There is security in drawing on the work of the past, and a lot can be learnt from studying historical pieces of embroidery, as well as other decorative arts. However, it is not enough to copy the technique or design elements from something like a 17th-century crewel work fire screen hoping that yours will have the same life and charm, without understanding the influences and reasons behind the choice of materials, colours, shapes and pattern that were used. Every period has its own values and standards, and what was appropriate in the 17th century may not be so today. The 20th century esteems discovery, experimentation and self-expression, which is a daunting and sobering thought for even the most skilled craftsman. But experimentation and self-expression, however clever and imaginative, must not be an excuse for poor standards of workmanship. In this matter the professionalism of the past sets an example.

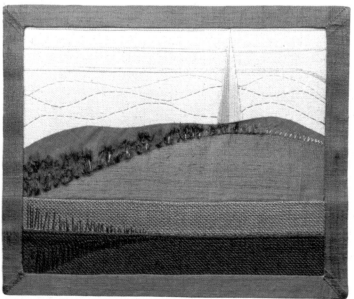

1. 'Summer' worked on Welsh wool flannel with appliquéd fabrics and couched laid threads. Flowers and grasses are in stem, satin and chain stitch, bullion and French knots.

2. 'Winter' worked on linen with appliquéd hessian. Threads include knitting yarn and gold thread; the hills and clouds are in simple running stitch.

William Morris (1834–96) was a designer who appreciated this to the extent of unpicking old embroideries in order to find out exactly how they had been put together. Thus he could execute his own designs with the same precision and sensitivity that he admired in the earlier work.

DESIGN SOURCES

Where do we get our inspiration? It is not a matter of simply waiting for an idea to appear miraculously in one's mind. It is an *awareness* which comes first from a knowledge of one's craft and second from looking at the world about us, recognizing and absorbing those elements that stimulate the mind to begin the design process.

A design might evolve from handling various fabrics and discovering a particularly attractive print. A printed fabric can serve admirably as a basis for embroidery. Or inspiration may come in a flash while you are walking down the street, or looking through a magazine. Something sparks off a thought; for example, a group of leafless trees in autumn may conjure up an image of interwoven vertical and diagonal lines, perhaps in various colours. Next comes the hard work of externalizing and giving shape to something that exists only as a fragile mental picture. The way in which this is carried out is personal and unique for each of us, and each will discover and develop his or her own methods.

PREPARATION AND ARRANGEMENT

Try out various media to find out which you can most easily manage and which you feel confident in using and manipulating. Try drawing—even if it means only a few line sketches—or painting. Or cut shapes from paper. Coloured paper and newsprint can prove extremely helpful when you are trying to balance one shape or area against another. For example, if your mental picture has a geometric quality, cut out a variety of simple shapes and place them on a piece of paper or fabric on which you have marked the outer edge of the work. Arrange and rearrange the shapes until you are satisfied with the design. Try all possibilities and beware of becoming satisfied too quickly. Take tracings of each arrangement so that you can refer to them and compare one with another.

During this discovery process you may feel the need to alter the shape and size of some of the elements or of the whole design. The background area of a design and the design elements that are contained within it influence one another and cannot be considered separately. However, if the finished article is to be a functional object such as a chair cover, cushion or lampshade, the size will already be established. It sometimes helps to make a facsimile of the design—such as a coloured tracing—and place it *in situ* to see how it looks relative to its surroundings. If the size of the object is a variable, deciding on the appropriate size may be difficult. Simply considering the matter may stimulate new ideas and lead one to produce something quite different from the original idea. A design that was originally conceived as a large wall hanging may work better as a small circular panel and vice versa. The size can also influence the choice of technique. The beauty of crewel work will be lost on a very small design, whereas fine whitework may be unsuitable for a very large object.

Once having decided on the size of the design area, consider the way in which the contained space is divided up by the design elements. There are few rules to follow and decisions regarding proportion of a shape or area of space, or of one line to another are made by 'eye', by aesthetic sensibility. You will develop a feel for what is right and wrong for your particular concept. To obtain a simple understanding of this, try dividing up a given area—25 × 20 cm (8 × 10 in)—using line and colour. (See examples 1, 2 and 3 above.)

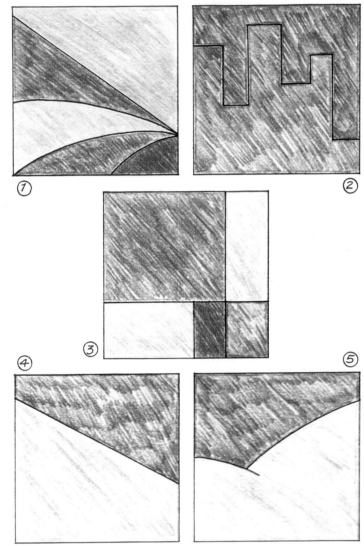

Try not to divide up an area too evenly; this can feel static and boring. For example, if you are planning a landscape design, this may require a horizon line and you will have to decide where to place this line within the design area. Begin by dividing the area into two (see examples 4 and 5 above).

Keep these experiments as reference. Decide which arrangements 'work' and why, and which do not 'work' and why. Which arrangements are visually satisfying? Which create feelings of movement? of tranquillity?

Whatever shapes are used within the design, remember that the spaces between and around them are just as important to the balance of the whole as the shapes themselves. This applies when the design is an overall repeat pattern as well as when there is a focal point or main area of interest. In order to see the background space more clearly, colour it in to make a negative of the design, and see if the shape thus created appears awkward or remains cohesive. You may feel that the background area should be reduced in order that other elements gain dominance, or for the effect to be more balanced.

As long as you are aware of points that might require change, it is not absolutely necessary to make every decision before you begin stitching. In fact it will be impossible to do so if the work is to grow freely. You will learn far more by leaving some things to chance. For example, the background space could be altered by the introduction of simple lines of stitchery which will break up the area and add interest without interfering too much with the already-existing design elements. Remember also that other elements can lead the eye into and around the main area of interest.

Design harmony results from an awareness of balance and proportion, and also of the unifying qualities of shape. If too many different kinds of shape are used together, the design may look disjointed. On the other hand, the 'feel' of a shape or line can be echoed within other elements without being repetitious, and can be complemented by the introduction of a single contrasting element.

In the design sketch (example 6 above) the curves of the foliage forms echo the curves of the architecture, which are balanced by the straight lines. These in turn provide a framework on which the eye can rest. The design thus contains movement and rest, the one merging into the other.

COLOUR

Design harmony also relies on the successful use of colour. This is another hurdle to overcome by questions and experimentation. Often people are afraid to rely on their own colour sense and need a lot of encouragement to take a risk. Yet we are surrounded by colour and are constantly choosing and discriminating for ourselves, albeit unconsciously.

Start by looking at the colours of objects in your home. Walk from room to room and analyze the colours and how they have been used. Look at your own clothes. Why have you chosen

some colours and not others? Is it because they complement the colour of your skin, eyes or hair, or because they make you feel warm or confident? Already you are using colour for a purpose. Collect samples of fabrics and threads and try to analyze and name each colour as accurately as you can. You will find that a pure red, yellow or blue is hard to find. Colour is much more complicated than our language can suggest. What, for example, is 'yellow-green'? The answer will involve recognizing the proportions of yellow to green, without which the description 'yellow-green' will imply a different colour to different people. With a keen awareness of colour we can discover a vast world of design possibilities.

Observe natural objects. The bark of a tree may be described as brown, but not if we are really looking hard. The 'brown' may be composed of hundreds of tones of colour ranging from green to purple to yellow, and yet they all work harmoniously together. Why? The 'green' may be made up of purple and yellow, the purple may contain green, and the yellow, purple and so on, each influencing the other. In the same way a predominantly 'red' painting may contain orange-red, blue-red and even pink (red plus white), so that many more colours are involved than at first appear, all combining and creating a certain effect.

The way we see colour depends on the nature of the light. If work is begun in daylight then all decisions regarding colour and threads must be done in daylight, as a change of lighting will alter the look of the materials quite dramatically. Remember also that silk and other smooth threads reflect light, making colours appear lighter when worked, whereas matt finish yarns, such as crewel wools, absorb light, making colours appear darker. The type of stitch can also affect the colour. The most extreme example is a pile stitch, in which the cut ends of yarn appear relatively dark, compared to the same yarn simply couched on the fabric surface.

To gain confidence in using contrasting and complementary colours together, choose a piece of fabric printed with a small design incorporating complementary colours, such as yellow and purple, red and green or blue and orange, and change the appearance of the fabric by covering an area or individual motifs with embroidery. Match the colours of the thread with those of the print and alter the original design balance by imposing one colour on another, creating larger areas of colour. Where the two contrasting colours are isolated in large areas their differences will be distinct, but where they are mingled in small dots or other details, they become blended, producing an impression of colour different from the individual components. Where detail is very fine, contrast is lost and the colours cancel each other out. Another illustration of this can be seen by comparing the bold contrast of black and white squares on a chessboard with the grey appearance of black and white arranged in fine lines.

TECHNIQUE

Before choosing threads and fabric, ask yourself whether the design is suitable for the technique you propose to use. This is where only experience can help you, and where working a sampler is so valuable. If your design consists of many curving, swirling lines it may be difficult to execute in counted thread work, which is basically made up of geometric filling stitches. A combination of two different techniques may be the answer. A design made up of many small shapes may not be suitable for metal thread work. It would be too fussy to execute with the neatness and precision necessary, as the threads would have to pass through the fabric too often and would be damaged. A design may, however, be interpreted in several different techniques. A variation of technique and a change of colour will alter the mood and feel of the original idea.

ENLARGING AND REDUCING THE SIZE OF A DESIGN

When your designing process is complete—apart from minor changes while stitching—you will have put it, in some form, on paper. It may be in the form of a drawing, or a tracing taken from experiments with cut-out paper. If it is the correct size then the design can be transferred immediately to the fabric.

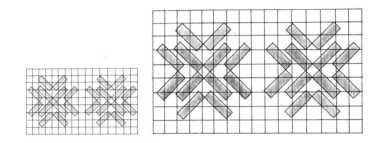

Often, however, it is more convenient to plan the design to a smaller scale than that of the finished work. Or, conversely, your design source—say a photograph—may be larger than the work is to be. The usual method of enlarging or decreasing the size of a design is by squaring it. First trace the design and then divide the tracing into equal squares with a coloured pencil and a ruler. Take another piece of paper and draw on it the same number of squares, making them larger or smaller by the required proportion. That is, if you want the design to be twice as large as the original, the squares must be twice the size of those on the tracing. Onto this grid draw in the design, copying the original carefully, square by square.

TRANSFERRING A DESIGN ONTO FABRIC

The fabric must be stable and completely flat, preferably mounted in a frame. The following three methods require a tracing of the design, as it is always wise to keep the original drawing or other source material as reference while working the embroidery. If it is difficult to see all the lines of the drawing through the tracing paper, lay both on a light box, or piece of glass or clear plastic held over a lamp. The light will make the design shine through the tracing paper, enabling you to make a quick, accurate copy. A design can be taken from a photographic transparency by shining the image through a projector onto paper pinned to the wall. The size of the image can be altered by moving the projector and focus.

1. Transferring with carbon paper

You will need: Dressmaker's carbon paper—dark for light fabrics, light for dark fabrics
Tracing paper
Pencil

Lay the carbon paper between the fabric and tracing and draw over the design lines with a sharp pencil. The fabric should be held square, but a bit slack, in the frame and placed on a table to provide a hard surface. The fabric can be tensioned after the design has been transferred. This carbon method is as accurate as the following traditional one.

2. Pricking and pouncing

You will need: Powdered tailor's chalk
A thick pin or needle for pricking
Tracing paper
Marking pen or oil paint and fine brush
Pad or cloth or rolled felt for applying the chalk
A square of felt

Choose a colour of tailor's chalk ('pounce') that will show on the fabric. Lay the tracing on top of the square of felt and, with the pin or needle, make perforations along the lines of the drawing. Holes should be close together so that details of the drawing will show through. Pin the pricked design onto the framed fabric. Dip the pad or rolled felt into the powdered chalk and dab

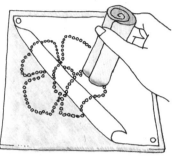

it over the tracing, forcing chalk through the holes and onto the fabric. Remove the tracing carefully. Fix the design by painting over the pounce spots with oil paint or by drawing with a fine indelible marking pen.

The disadvantage of these first two methods is that the design, once fixed, cannot be altered, and the marked outlines must be entirely covered by the stitchery. It is unsuitable on very fine or transparent fabrics, or those with a pile.

3. Tacking [basting] method

This does not permanently mark the fabric and is cleaner than the last two methods. It is suitable for use on all types of material. Its greatest advantage is that the embroiderer is left with flexibility to alter the design as it takes shape during working, which is often necessary if the work is original. Its only disadvantage is that fine details of design cannot be reproduced as accurately as with the other methods.

You will need: Tracing paper
Ordinary sewing thread
Needle

Frame the fabric and pin the tracing onto it. Tack [baste] over the outlines, using small stitches to retain as much detail as possible. Run the point of a needle gently along the tacked lines. This will score the paper, making it easier to tear away piece by piece, leaving the tacked design on the fabric. Do not pull sharply on the paper or the stitches will become dis-

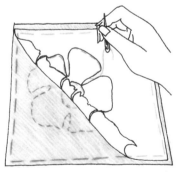

torted. The thread used should match the fabric in colour as closely as possible without being too difficult to see. The embroidery stitches may cover the thread completely, but if they do not, bits that cannot be removed will not be visible.

Now you are ready to begin. All the hard work of preparation means that the first stitch can be made with a measure of confidence. There will still be decisions to be made, however, and one of the last and most difficult is knowing exactly when to stop. View the work from a distance and from all angles. Isolate it from the distractions of surroundings by making a paper frame in which to see it clearly. If uncertain, leave the work until you can view it with a fresh eye. Good design has nothing superfluous about it; everything within it should make a constructive contribution to the whole.

'COTTAGE CHRYSANTHEMUMS'

This charming still-life of a vase of flowers makes effective use of a variety of simple embroidery stitches and is a rewarding project for a beginner to tackle.

MATERIALS

1 skein each of Anchor Stranded Cotton [six-strand embroidery floss] in each of the following 20 colours: canary yellow 0291, buttercup 0292, buttercup 0293, buttercup 0297, buttercup 0298, (i.e. progressively darker shades), orange 0323, parrot green 0256, emerald 0229, apple green 0204, flame 0332, gorse yellow 0302, amber gold 0306, chestnut 0349 and (darker) 0351, cinnamon 0369, scarlet 046, grey 0397 and (darker) 0400, almond green 0262, parrot green 0258. (If this brand is not available, match the colours as closely as possible to the colour photograph.)

A piece of calico [unbleached cotton] 36 × 40 cm (14 × 16 in); white cotton tape 16 mm ($\frac{3}{4}$ in) wide; crewel needles; pins; a round embroidery frame; tracing paper; dressmaker's carbon paper; stiff card [cardboard] backing measuring 20 × 24 cm (8 × 9$\frac{1}{2}$ in) and strong thread for mounting the finished embroidery.

Size
Approximately 14 × 18 cm (5$\frac{1}{2}$ × 7 in).

To prepare the fabric
Keeping the grain of the fabric straight, stretch the calico [unbleached cotton] tightly in the embroidery frame. Trace the design from the diagram. Position the design centrally on the calico [unbleached cotton]. Place the dressmaker's carbon paper, ink side down, between the design and the calico [unbleached cotton]. Pin the tracing and the carbon paper in position. Put a small thick book in the frame recess and, using a ball-point pen, transfer the design to the calico [unbleached cotton]. If your embroidery hoop is too small to allow you to transfer the entire design, do it in 2 stages but be careful to avoid distortion.

To work the embroidery
(Refer to the Stitch Glossary for instructions on how to work the individual stitches.) Work the embroidery in the following order.

Using 1 strand of buttercup 0292, work the diagonal *window* bars in long and short stitch. Using 2 strands of buttercup 0292, work the window uprights and sill in satin stitch, and the bottom of the window frame in long and short stitch.

Outline the *curtains* in stem

4mm margin all round to allow for adjustment of finished picture when framing.

stitch, using 1 strand of buttercup 0293. Using single strands of buttercup 0292, buttercup 0297 and buttercup 0298, work the detached chain stitches which form the pattern on the curtains.

Using 1 strand of orange 0323, work the diagonal lines on the *wallpaper*, making 1 long back stitch for each side of each diamond. At each intersection make one lazy daisy with 5 petals, using 1 strand of buttercup 0298.

With 1 strand of buttercup 0293, outline the far edge of the *tablecloth* in stem stitch. Using 1 strand each of orange 0323, parrot green 0256, buttercup 0297 and emerald 0229, work the tablecloth checks in small running stitch.

Using 2 strands of buttercup 0292, work the *window 'stay'* by making a row of small chain stitches within the outline. Then whip the chain stitches without piercing the fabric behind. Work the prong and the window fastener in the same way.

Using 2 strands of apple green 0204, work a row of chain stitch between the lines making the base of the *vase*. Cover this with sloping satin stitch to give a raised effect. Work the rim of the vase in the same way. Using 1 strand of apple green 0204, outline the body of the vase in split stitch, and fill in with vertical rows of split stitch following the shape of the vase.

Using double strands of orange 0323, flame 0332, gorse yellow 0302, buttercup 0297 and 0293, canary yellow 0291 and buttercup 0298, work the *flower* petals in filled lazy daisy (inserting a straight stitch in each). Using single strands of chestnut 0351, amber gold 0306, cinnamon 0369 and chestnut 0349, work the flower centres in French knots. Work the leaves in concentric rows of stem stitches, using double strands of parrot green 0256, parrot green 0258 and almond green 0262. Use the same colours in double strands and work the flower sepals in lazy daisy stitch, and the stems in stem stitch. Work the closed buds in circular

buttonhole stitch. Fill in any unwanted gaps between the flowers with leaves or buds.

Using 2 strands of scarlet 046, work the *scissor* handles in the same way as the window 'stay'. Finally, using single strands of grey 0397 and 0400, work the scissor blades in split stitch.

To finish
Remove the embroidery from the frame.

If necessary, first wash the embroidery gently by hand to remove any remaining design marks. Press lightly using a cloth.

Pin the cotton tape all around the edge of the calico [unbleached cotton] so that it does not extend beyond the edge. Machine stitch in place with 3 rows of zig-zags. Using strong thread, lace the picture tightly across the card [cardboard] pulling it into shape (see instructions on page 17). The embroidery is now ready for framing.

Bead and Sequin Work

Beads are used for decoration all over the world. Any material which can have a hole pierced through it can serve as a bead or be made into one. Seeds and seed pods, bones, pebbles and shells can make natural beads; clay, glass, wood, metal and papier mâché are some of the materials often used for man-made ones. The most prized, of course, are real gems and semi-precious stones. In many cultures beads have been symbols of wealth and status and have even been used as currency. And from early times they have also been used in embroidery, to create sumptuous decoration on costumes and costume accessories, purses, pincushions, boxes, fire screens, panels and bookcovers. Beads are usually light in weight, but when many are applied to a fabric the weight of the article can be considerably increased. The ground fabric, therefore, must be of sufficient strength to support both beads and stitchery.

The earliest sequins or spangles were made of beaten gold and silver in a variety of shapes, from domed circles to squares, stars and crescent moons. Now they are almost always made of plastic and come in an enormous range of colours. They can be bought either separately or strung in a row on cotton thread.

To apply beads

Before beginning to work, sort beads and sequins by size and colour and keep them separate in small containers. Use a piece of felt or velvet as a working surface when sorting and threading them, to prevent them from rolling about. Use a long, fine beading needle and a thread which has first been run through beeswax. This helps the beads to slide easily onto the thread and prevents it from becoming frayed. If the bead hole is too fine for a needle, wax the end of the thread well and roll it to a point, which will then pass through the hole.

There are several ways of applying beads to fabric:

Method 1 The simplest method of applying beads at random in free embroidery is to sew each one down individually. Bring the needle up through the fabric and thread on a bead. Insert the needle back through the same hole and bring it up again where the next bead is required. This method was used frequently in stump work, a type of raised embroidery popular in 17th-century England; the beads were applied as closely as possible with no sense of direction. In modern embroidery a beautiful filling can be created with a combination of beads, seeding and French knots.

Method 1.

Method 2 Bring the needle up through the fabric and thread on a few beads, then take a small stitch through the ground fabric to secure them in place before threading on more beads. This

method was used by North American Indian tribes —often on leather—and is known as lazy squaw stitch.

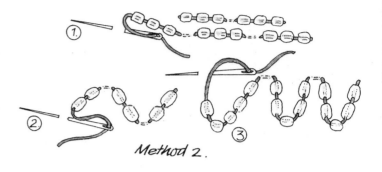

Method 2.

Method 3 Couching may be used to apply rows of beads. Bring the needle through, thread a row of beads and lay them on the fabric. Use a separate needle and thread for couching. Bring the couching thread up through the fabric and make an overcast stitch over the laid thread between each bead. Slide the beads close together after each stitch until the whole row is secured. Take the end of the laid thread to the underside and fasten off.

This method is ideal when long strands of one colour are required or when forming a pattern in which the beads need to lie neatly in one direction. If the beads are of uniform size, patterns can be worked out on graph paper, with each square representing one bead. The number and placing of coloured beads in each row is then followed closely when threading up, and the pattern reproduced exactly on the fabric. This method can also be used for attaching loops of beads; the beads are threaded onto metal thread or thin wire, which is then couched down at intervals with loops formed between stitches.

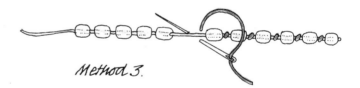

Method 3.

Method 4 Loops, tassels and fringes can be made from long strings of beads. When forming a loose fringe, take the thread through and around the last bead at the bottom of each row, and bring it back up through the beads to the top, so that a double thread supports the weight.

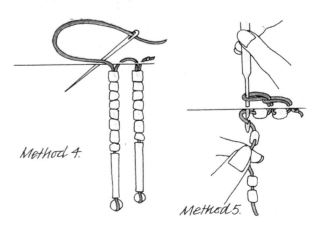

Method 4.

Method 5.

Method 5 Beads can be applied using a tambour hook. The linear design is drawn on the reverse side of the fabric, which is held taut, wrong side up, in a frame. The beads are first threaded, and then held under the frame with one hand while the other hand pushes the hook down through the fabric, picking up the beginning of the thread. A loop is then drawn up through the fabric and the first bead pushed up to rest below the fabric. The hook is inserted again just ahead of the first bead, and another loop brought up through the first loop, so securing the bead. With practice this becomes an extremely quick method; it is one which is used commercially.

To apply sequins
Sequins are generally applied individually, the stitching being either invisible or part of the decoration.

Method 1 Bring the needle up and insert it through the eye of the sequin. Work a back stitch to the right over the sequin, emerging to the left of it, half the sequin's diameter away. Thread on the next sequin, which should lie edge to edge with the previous one.

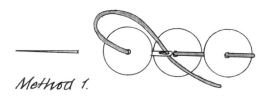

Method 1.

Method 2 Begin as for Method 1 but bring the needle out at the left edge of the sequin after the first back stitch, and make a second back stitch through the eye of the sequin before proceeding to the next.

For an extra decorative touch, sequins can be stitched down with a bead or a bit of twisted metal thread—called a purl—slipped onto the needle before each back stitch is worked.

Method 2.

Method 3 The sequins are applied here with back stitches worked over the left side, so that the right side overlaps the previous one, hiding the previous stitch. If rows are worked close together the ground fabric will also be hidden, producing an extremely rich effect.

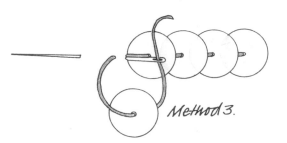

Method 3.

Beaded jacket

See photograph on page 43.
MATERIALS
Purchased commercial pattern for jacket; cream fabric (because the beads are quite heavy when used in concentrated areas, a fine lightweight fabric may need to be interlined); lining fabric; beads in the following 4 colours: transparent, gold, silver and pale coral; 3 mm mother of pearl sequins; gold thread; one skein each of Anchor stranded cotton [six-strand embroidery floss] in buttercup 0293 and peach 9575 (if this brand is not available, match the colours as closely as possible to the colour photograph); sewing thread to match fabric; a beading needle; pins and crewel needles; a large rectangular embroidery frame; dressmaker's squared paper or graph paper; tracing paper; dressmaker's carbon paper (optional).

To prepare the fabric
All of the beading must be worked before the jacket is stitched. Mark the jacket fronts around the stitching lines on the right side of the fabric using tacking [basting] stitches, but do not cut them out. Cut out a rectangle of fabric enclosing each front. Mount the right front on a large frame. The beading is worked much more easily when the frame is supported leaving both hands free to manipulate the beads. Next enlarge both motifs on page 42; 10 squares on the paper represent 2.5 cm (1 in). Trace the enlarged motifs. Transfer the large motif onto the right side of the right front. This can be

done either by the dressmaker's carbon method *or* by tacking [basting] the outline through the tracing paper (see page 37). Leave at least 1.5 cm ($\frac{5}{8}$ in) between the motif and the seam line.

To embroider the fabric
(Refer to the Stitch Glossary for instructions on how to work the individual stitches.) The beads should be applied to the fabric with a running stitch (fig. 1), keeping the spaces between the beads even. Use either the sewing thread or the gold thread (the transparent beads look quite effective when held down by gold thread) with the beading needle. Bead the outlines of the flowers first. Then work the clusters of beads and sequins. The sequins should be applied so that they overlap slightly (see left). Using 3 strands of stranded cotton [embroidery floss], work the French knots and the straight stitches. Embroider the stems and the leaves with the gold thread, using any line stitch. On the jacket shown, chain stitch is used for the stems and outlines, back stitch for the leaf veins.

To finish
When the embroidery has been completed, remove the fabric from the frame and using the pattern as a guide, cut out the jacket front. (The beading may have 'taken up' a little fabric.) Mount the second jacket front and work in the same way as the first, but using the smaller motif. Make up the jacket following the instructions given with the pattern.

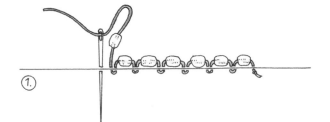

①.

BEADED JACKET
BEADED COMBS

The scope of bead and sequin work is illustrated by these very different but equally eye-catching designs. The addition of beads and sequins lifts a simple evening jacket into the world of haute couture while the beaded combs would add a sparkle to any occasion.

▬ Gold thread		▬ Stranded cotton	
▬ Sequins		▬ Stranded cotton	
▬ Silver beads		⣿ French knots	
▬ Gold beads		⣀ French knots	
▬ Transparent beads		═ Straight stitch	
▬ Pale coral beads			

10 squares 2·5cm (1in)

CHEVRON CUSHION COVER

The basic chevron design is interpreted in many different stitches on this unusual cushion cover in shades of pink. Narrow ribbon is incorporated to add texture.

MATERIALS

2 pieces of medium-weight, natural-coloured fabric 46 cm (18 in) square; thick embroidery thread (cottons and linens) in the following 4 colours—pale pink, dusty pink, rose pink and bright pink; buttonhole-twist in burgundy; sewing thread to match fabric; tacking [basting] thread; 3 m ($3\frac{1}{2}$ yd) of 3 mm ($\frac{1}{8}$ in) wide burgundy satin ribbon; an embroidery frame; pins; crewel needles; 2 m ($2\frac{1}{4}$ yd) of 2.5 cm (1 in) wide burgundy satin ribbon for piping; a ready-made cushion [pillow] 46 cm (18 in) square; graph paper; and tissue paper.

Size

The finished size of the cushion [pillow] is 43 cm (17 in) square.

To prepare the fabric

Overcast the raw edges of the fabric by hand or machine. Mark the centre of one of the fabric squares with tacking [basting] at A (see diagram). Tack [baste] 1.3 cm ($\frac{1}{2}$ in) in from the edge along all 4 sides to mark the seam allowance. The 26 stitch guide lines will fit within this inner area. Enlarge pattern repeat (10 squares on the diagram = 2.5 cm/1 in) and copy the pattern onto tissue paper. (See page 37 for enlarging instructions.) Mount the fabric in the frame and transfer the guide lines onto it, working tacking [basting] stitches through the tissue. Remove the tissue.

To embroider the fabric

(Refer to the Stitch Glossary for instructions on how to work the individual stitches.) For the embroidery, complete all the lines worked in one stitch before moving on to the next as follows:
On line 1 work feather stitch in dusty pink along the zig-zag. Then, on top of the same line, work chained feather stitch in rose pink.
On lines 2 and 8 work 4 running stitches in rose pink along each straight chevron side, and complete by threading the fine burgundy ribbon through these stitches.
On lines 3 and 7 work double running or back stitch in dusty pink.
On lines 4 and 6 work Pekinese stitch using rose pink for the base stitch and pale pink for the interlacing thread.
On line 5 work chained feather stitch with the burgundy thread. On line 9 work double running stitch in pale pink and dusty pink.
On lines 10 and 12 work cable chain stitch in bright pink.
On line 11 work open cretan stitch in the burgundy thread to run between lines 10 and 12.
On line 13 work chained feather stitch in rose pink. Remove the guide lines.

To finish

When all the embroidery is completed, remove the fabric from the frame, and press lightly on the wrong side if necessary.
1. Fold the 2.5 cm (1 in) wide ribbon in half and tack [baste] the edges together 6 mm ($\frac{1}{4}$ in) in from the edge. Press flat (fig. 1).
Tack [baste] and stitch ribbon to right side of cushion [pillow], matching tacking [basting] line to seam line and placing the folded edge of the ribbon facing inwards. Tuck ends in at one corner. Snip the ribbon to ease curve (fig. 2).
2. With right sides together, tack [baste] and stitch remaining piece of fabric to cushion [pillow] front, leaving an opening on one edge.
3. Cut across corners of seam allowance and turn cushion [pillow] to the right side. Turn in remaining seam allowance and tack [baste]. Insert cushion [pillow] pad and slip stitch opening to close.

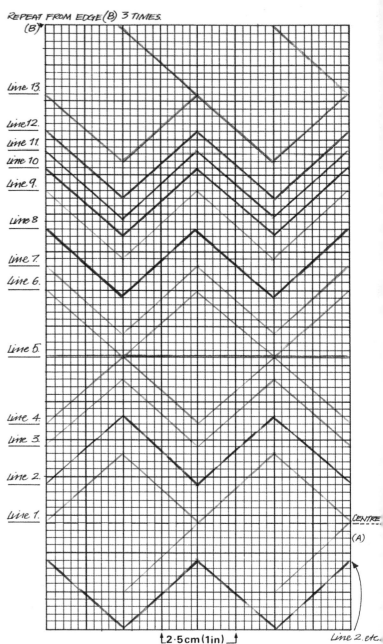

REPEAT FROM EDGE (B) 3 TIMES.
(B)
line 13.
line 12.
line 11.
line 10.
line 9.
line 8.
line 7.
line 6.
Line 5.
line 4.
line 3.
line 2.
Line 1.
CENTRE
(A)
2·5 cm (1 in)
Line 2. etc.

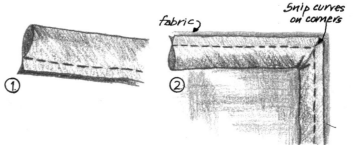

fabric

Snip curves on corners

① ②

46

Smocking

Smocking is a technique traditionally applied to clothing and used for holding the fullness of the fabric in a decorative manner. There is clear evidence of its having been practised throughout Western Europe since the 14th century. The farm worker's protective smock is perhaps the garment most associated with smocking, the cut and style being similar from country to country, though decorative details vary. These were usually made of rather coarse, hand-spun and hand-woven linen, on which it was comparatively simple to run in the gathering following the thread of the fabric. Yet smocking can be—and has been—applied to almost any fabric, fine or coarse, plain or patterned; and the stitches can be worked in an infinite variety of threads.

One of the first problems encountered by the beginner is deciding on the amount of material to allow for the smocking when cutting out a garment. This will vary depending on the fabric used, the depth of gathers and the stitch tension of the individual worker. It is best to begin by working a sampler on a small length of fabric and measuring it before and after smocking. The amount of decrease in the width will serve as a guide in cutting out the garment.

PREPARING THE FABRIC

Method 1 If an evenweave or check fabric is used, the length and spacing of the gathering stitches can be kept even by following the weave or pattern. Otherwise you can use a smocking transfer, which consists of rows of tiny dots, evenly spaced. Different transfers have dots spaced to suit different types of fabric. For example, if the material is as fine as crêpe de chine or muslin, a transfer with dots spaced 5 mm ($\frac{3}{16}$ in) apart is suitable. A coarser fabric requires a wider-spaced transfer. The transfer is ironed onto the wrong side of the fabric, with an allowance left for seams and finishing, and should follow the line of the weave as closely as possible.

A strong thread is needed for working the gathering stitches. Use a separate thread for each line and keep the lines about 1.2 cm ($\frac{1}{2}$ in) apart. Begin with a firm knot and a back stitch. Keep the stitches even by picking up the fabric at exactly the same intervals in each row. Leave the thread hanging at the end of each line of stitches. Once a sufficient number of lines have been worked, lay the fabric on a table and pull up the threads evenly. The resulting pleats should lie very close together but allow sufficient space for the needle to be inserted easily between them. Secure the ends of the gathering threads by twisting them around pins inserted into the fabric. The gathering threads should not be removed until all the smocking is finished. Use them as guide lines for the stitches.

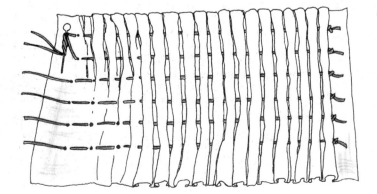

Method 2 This method is quicker than the first but requires practice. It is worked in a frame which supports the material, leaving both hands free to arrange the pleats and work the stitches.

First tie a long length of a very strong thread to a hook on the right-hand upright of the frame. Using this same thread, work one row of even gathering stitches across the fabric from selvedge to selvedge. Then pull tightly and tie the thread to a hook on the left upright.

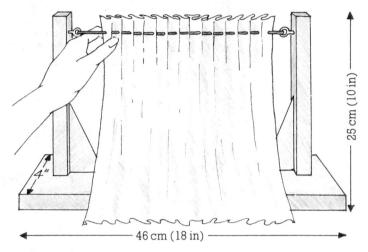

4"

25 cm (10 in)

46 cm (18 in)

While working the first row of smocking stitches, stroke the pleats in place using the first finger of the left hand behind the work and the thumb in front. This first row is usually outline stitch (sometimes called half cable stitch), which is easy to work directly under the gathering thread, from left to right. The first row of stitches will arrange and hold the pleats in place.

Begin by knotting the thread, then pass the needle through the double material of the first pleat at the back of the work. This will prevent the knot from coming through to the front. Bring the needle up between the first and second pleats on the right side to start the stitch. Finish the row with a couple of back stitches on the wrong side.

Continue with your chosen pattern of smocking stitches, leaving the fabric on the frame and controlling the pleats by hand as you go. It is a good idea to mark each selvedge with notches spaced at 2.5 cm (1 in) intervals to help keep the subsequent rows of smocking straight. As much as 15–20 cm (6–8 in) of smocking can be done on one gathering thread.

Work the following stitches from left to right unless otherwise instructed. Keep each stitch at an even tension throughout.

OUTLINE STITCH

This is the simplest of smocking stitches, and is recommended for the first row of any pattern. Use the same basic technique as for a surface stem stitch, picking up one pleat at a time. Keep the thread below the needle so that the stitches all slant in the same direction.

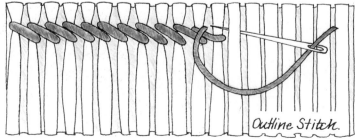

Outline Stitch.

CABLE STITCH

Bring the needle up on the left side of the first pleat. Pick up the next pleat from right to left, keeping the needle horizontal and the thread below it. Pick up the third pleat with the thread above the needle. Pick up the fourth with the thread below, and so on.

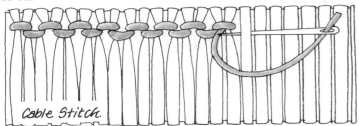

DOUBLE CABLE STITCH

Work two rows of cable stitch close together, one below the other.

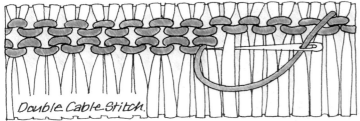

WAVE STITCH

Bring the needle up on the left side of a pleat. Pick up the next four pleats in turn with the thread *above* the needle, working each stitch slightly below the last, so forming a downward diagonal. Pick up the sixth pleat with the thread *below* the needle, and likewise work up four more stitches in turn, forming an upward diagonal. Pick up the tenth pleat with the thread *above* the needle and work as for the first diagonal.

Rows of wave stitch can be worked one below the other, as shown.

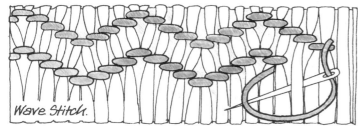

TRELLIS STITCH

Work two rows of wave stitch to form mirror images of each other with alternate points touching, as shown.

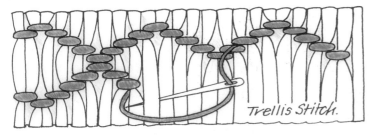

DIAMOND STITCH

Bring the needle up to the left of one pleat. Pick up the next pleat from right to left with the thread *below* the needle. Pick up the third pleat about 1 cm ($\frac{3}{8}$ in) higher up. Pick up the fourth pleat with the thread *above* the needle and the fifth pleat 1 cm ($\frac{3}{8}$ in) below this. Continue in this way. Work subsequent rows to form small diamond shapes.

HONEYCOMB STITCH

This is one of the quickest smocking stitches to execute. Work a double back stitch over two pleats, then pass the needle under the second pleat, up or down, approximately 1 cm ($\frac{3}{8}$ in), and join the second and third pleats with another double back stitch. Repeat the movement, alternating up and down along the row, working back stitches over the third and fourth, fourth and fifth, fifth and sixth pleats, and so on.

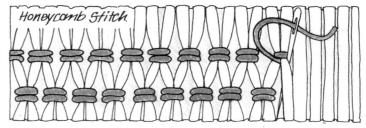

SURFACE HONEYCOMB–CHEVRON STITCH

This can be varied in depth and width and combined with other stitches in the same row. The diagonal stitch joining back stitches lies over the pleat or pleats instead of going through the pleat as for honeycomb stitch.

VANDYKE STITCH

Work from right to left. Make a back stitch through the first two pleats, then take the thread up, insert it under the second and third pleats and join them with a back stitch. Take the thread down and join the third and fourth pleats, and so on. This is a very strong smocking stitch.

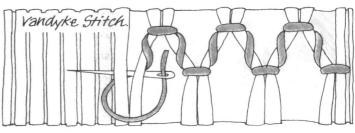

CHILD'S SMOCKED DRESS

Smocking looks particularly charming when used to decorate a special dress for a small girl. Several different smocking stitches have been used on the yoke of this dress, while embroidered scallops add detail to the collar and cuffs.

MATERIALS
1 skein each of Anchor stranded embroidery cotton [six-strand embroidery floss] in the following 4 colours:— carmine rose 040, white 0402, cobalt blue 0128, apple green 0204; and 2 skeins of carnation 024. (If this brand is not available, match the colours as closely as possible to the colour photograph.) 1.8 m (2 yd) of 115 cm (45 in) wide cotton lawn or similar light-weight fabric; 6 buttons 1 cm ($\frac{3}{8}$ in) in diameter; 2 small press studs [snaps]; strong thread; sewing thread to match fabric; 1.4 m (1$\frac{1}{2}$ yd) of 2.2 cm ($\frac{7}{8}$ in) wide pink ribbon; smocking dot transfer with dots and rows 6 mm ($\frac{1}{4}$ in) apart; pins; crewel needles; a pair of sharp embroidery scissors; and dressmaker's squared paper for pattern.

Size
The dress will fit a 56–58 cm (22–23 in) chest. The finished back length from nape of neck is 56 cm (22 in).

To make the pattern
Copy the pattern onto the dressmaker's squared paper, following the diagram (**fig. 1**). Two squares on the diagram represent 5 cm (2 in). A 1.3 cm ($\frac{1}{2}$ in) seam allowance and 17 cm (6$\frac{3}{4}$ in) hem have been included in the diagram pattern. Transfer all pattern markings.

Cutting out
Following the cutting layout (**fig. 1**), pin the pattern pieces onto the fabric and cut out the front and back only. Cut out the remaining pieces after completing the smocking on the front and back. Transfer all pattern markings.

Smocking preparation
Prepare a length of smocking dots 110 × 13 cm (43$\frac{1}{4}$ × 5$\frac{1}{4}$ in) for front and 2 lengths of dots 55.5 × 4 cm (22 × 1$\frac{1}{2}$ in) for the back. Join transfers on the back if necessary with adhesive [masking] tape.

Press all creases out of front and back pieces. Pin smocking dots to wrong side of front, placing the top row of dots 6 mm ($\frac{1}{4}$ in) above seamline. Iron dots off.

Repeat for back, leaving 1.3 cm ($\frac{1}{2}$ in) gap at centre.

To work the gathers
Work the rows of gathering stitches, working from top to bottom. Make a knot at the end of a length of strong thread and work a tiny back stitch on the first dot. Work across the row, picking up 2 threads of the fabric of each

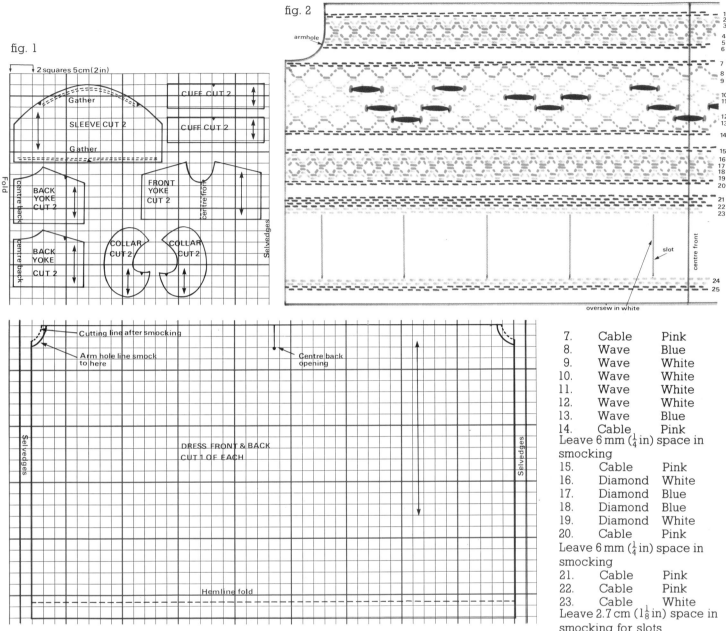

fig. 1

fig. 2

Row	Stitch	Colour
7.	Cable	Pink
8.	Wave	Blue
9.	Wave	White
10.	Wave	White
11.	Wave	White
12.	Wave	White
13.	Wave	Blue
14.	Cable	Pink

Leave 6 mm ($\frac{1}{4}$ in) space in smocking

15.	Cable	Pink
16.	Diamond	White
17.	Diamond	Blue
18.	Diamond	Blue
19.	Diamond	White
20.	Cable	Pink

Leave 6 mm ($\frac{1}{4}$ in) space in smocking

21.	Cable	Pink
22.	Cable	Pink
23.	Cable	White

Leave 2.7 cm ($1\frac{1}{8}$ in) space in smocking for slots

24.	Cable	White
25.	Cable	Pink

Work bullion knot rose buds in pink and rose over white wave stitching (lines 9–12). Work detached chain stitch leaves in green each side of buds.

DRESS BACK

Row	Stitch	Colour
1.	Cable	Pink
2.	Cable	White
3.	Diamond	Blue
4.	Diamond	Blue
5.	Diamond	White
6.	Cable	Pink

Leave 6 mm ($\frac{1}{4}$ in) space in smocking

7.	Cable	Pink
8.	Wave	Blue

dot only. Leave a short length of thread free at end of row.

Work the gathering rows right across for the front. On the back, work 2 sets of gathers leaving a 1.3 cm ($\frac{1}{2}$ in) gap at the centre for the opening. Pull up all the gathers evenly but not too tightly, and secure the thread ends in pairs by winding them in a figure of 8 around a pin inserted at the end of the rows.

These gathers must stay in until all the smocking has been completed.

To work the smocking stitches
Work the smocking following the diagram (**fig. 2**) leaving 1.3 cm ($\frac{1}{2}$ in) free at the edges. (See pages 48–49 for instructions on how to work the various smocking stitches.) Use 3 strands of embroidery cotton throughout. Leave a space for working the slots for threading the ribbon through as shown. When the smocking is complete on the front and back, work the slots as follows.

Using pins, mark 10 equally spaced slot positions across the space left unworked in the smocking on the dress front. Cut slots large enough to thread ribbon through easily.

Roll raw edge of slot slightly to wrong side and overcast firmly.

Cut armhole shapings on front and back as indicated on pattern.

Stitches and colours used for smocking:
DRESS FRONT

Row	Stitch	Colour
1.	Cable	Pink
2.	Diamond	White
3.	Diamond	Blue
4.	Diamond	Blue
5.	Diamond	White
6.	Cable	Pink

Leave 6 mm ($\frac{1}{4}$ in) space in smocking

51

SAMPLER

SWEDISH CUSHION COVER

These traditional designs use quite different techniques. The cross stitch sampler has a geometric feel while the cushion cover uses stitches to create flowing curves.

10 squares 2·5cm (1in)

Key

	0302 Gorse Yellow	019 Cardinal Red
0140 Electric Blue	0369 Cinnamon	0382 Coffee
0131 Cobalt Blue	0266 Moss Green	0371 Cinnamon
0109 Parma Violet	0244 Grass Green	0368 Cinnamon

XX Cross stitch

— Double running stitch

∨ Fly stitch

||||| Satin stitch

'SUMMER BEEHIVE'
'HERBACEOUS BORDER'

Hot summer days are conjured up by these delightful little pictures worked with colour and texture in mind. The background fabric is painted to add depth to the scenes, and the stitches are carefully chosen to give a realistic look to the flowers.

Rope Stitch.

TABLE NAPKINS
PINCUSHION

The delicate-looking organdie table napkins (below) are decorated with a form of shadow work. The pincushion (right) is heavily embroidered with raised stitches to give a relief effect.

Shadow work table napkins

MATERIALS
For each napkin: 45 cm (18 in) square of white organdie; piece of bright-coloured cotton lawn or batiste, approximately 12 cm (5 in) square, and 1 skein of stranded embroidery cotton [six-strand embroidery floss] to match; tacking [basting] thread; tracing paper; a soft pencil; a pair of sharp embroidery scissors; pins; crewel needles; a 13 cm (5 in) round embroidery frame; and bias binding for binding the frame.

Size
Approximately 43 cm (17 in) square.

To prepare the fabric
Trace the motif onto the tracing paper. Fold the organdie into 4 diagonally, to find the centre and provide a guide for placing the motif. Place the tracing paper under the organdie, on a flat surface, so that the stalk of the flower lies along one of the diagonal folds. The motif can be moved along the fold as required, but at least a 4 cm (1½ in) margin should be left between the edges of the leaves and the edges of the organdie. Pin the organdie onto the tracing paper and trace the motif onto the fabric with the pencil. Unpin the tracing paper.

Lay the organdie on the coloured fabric so that the motif lies in the centre, making sure that the threads of both fabrics lie in the same direction. Keeping both fabrics flat, pin and then tack [baste] them together, leaving a small margin between the traced motif and the tacking [basting].

Bind the inner ring of the embroidery frame with the bias binding. Place the inner ring under the 2 layers of fabric and press the outer ring over them, tightening the screw. Make sure that both layers of fabric are pulled drum-tight and that the organdie is uppermost.

To embroider the fabric
(Refer to the Stitch Glossary for instructions on how to work the individual stitches.) Work the motif through both layers of fabric, omitting the stalk and the centre petal. Use 2 strands of embroidery thread throughout. For the flower, work the 2 inner petals in stem stitch and the 2 outer petals in chain stitch. Work around each leaf with overcast stitch and then stitch the veins in back stitch.

Remove the frame and cut away the spare lawn with sharp scissors. Great care is needed to cut close to the stitching without cutting the stitches themselves. Work the remaining petal in double back stitch (see herringbone stitch on page 22), beginning at the base and working round until the stitches meet at the top. Work the stalk in whipped chain stitch.

To finish
Press the work carefully under a clean damp cloth.

To finish the edge, roll a narrow hem and stitch in the normal way. Alternatively, turn under 1.2–2 cm (½–¾ in) all round to make a single hem, mitring the corners. Pin and tack [baste]. Work a line of chain stitch, or overcast stitch, 1.2 cm (½ in) from the edge (if needed, draw a guide line). Cut the organdie on the wrong side close to the stitching. Slip stitch the corners.

Note: A very fine, delicate effect can be obtained by using white organdie instead of coloured lawn and stitching it in white thread. The 2 layers of transparent material give a 'watered' effect.

CHRISTENING GOWN AND BONNET

MATERIALS

2 m ($2\frac{1}{4}$ yd) of 115 cm (44/45 in) wide white cotton lawn; white sewing thread; 3 skeins of white stranded embroidery cotton [embroidery floss]; tacking [basting] thread; six 1 cm ($\frac{3}{8}$ in) white buttons; ball of No. 40 white mercerized crochet cotton for buttonhole loops; 1.7 m ($1\frac{3}{4}$ yd) of narrow white lace for skirt; 1.7 m ($1\frac{3}{4}$ yd) of 1.2 cm ($\frac{1}{2}$ in) wide white satin ribbon; pins; crewel needles; dressmaker's squared paper for pattern; and an embroidery frame with a stand.

Size

This dress will fit a child with a chest measurement up to 46 cm (18 in).

To make the pattern

Copy the pattern onto the dressmaker's squared paper, following the diagram (**fig. 1a**). Two squares on the diagram represent 5 cm (2 in). A seam allowance of 1.3 cm ($\frac{1}{2}$ in) has been included on all edges in the diagram pattern and a hem of 3.5 cm ($1\frac{3}{8}$ in). Transfer all pattern markings.

Cutting out

Following the cutting layout (**fig. 1b**), pin the pattern pieces onto the fabric and cut out the skirt, 2 sleeves, 2 cuffs, 2 frills, 2 bodice backs, 2 bodice back facings and the bodice front facing only. Transfer all pattern markings.

To prepare the fabric

Tack [baste] around the outlines of the remaining pieces—bodice front, 2 cuffs, bonnet back and bonnet front. Remove the pattern. Mount the fabric with the outlines on a free standing frame.

1a

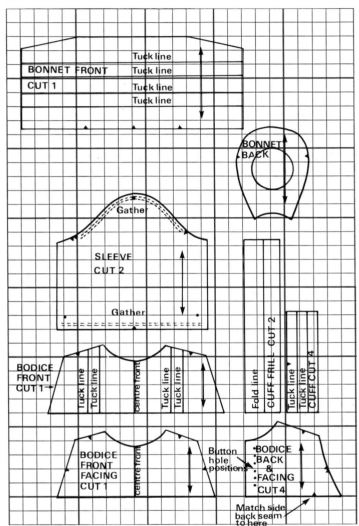

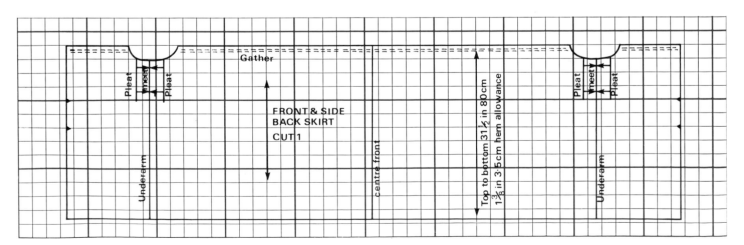

Embroidery Supplies

UNITED KINGDOM
The following sell embroidery supplies by mail order:

Royal School of Needlework
25 Princes Gate
Kensington
London SW7 1QE
Tel: 01 589 0077

DeDenne Ltd
159/161 Kenton Road
Kenton
Harrow, Middlesex
Tel: 01 907 5476

**The Campden Needlecraft
Centre**
High Street
Chipping Campden
Gloucestershire
Tel: Evesham (0386) 840583

The Handicraft Shop
5 Oxford Road
Altrincham
Cheshire
Tel: 061 928 3834

Louis Grosse Ltd
Mail Order Department
Wyddial Hall
Buntingford
Herts

Ruth John
39 The Square
Titchfield
Hampshire
Tel: (03294) 46186

Mace & Nairn
89 Crane Street
Salisbury
Wiltshire SP1 2PY
Tel: (0722) 6903
(International mail order)

Stitches
30a St Leonard's Road
Windsor
Berkshire
Tel: (95) 68068

The Silver Thimble
33 Gay Street
Bath
Avon BA1 2NT
Tel: (0225) 23457

UNITED STATES
The following nationwide chain stores usually stock a good
selection of embroidery supplies:

**Ben Franklin Stores; Jefferson Stores; Kay Mart; M H Lamston;
J C Penney Stores; Sears Roebuck; Woolworth's.**

The following sell embroidery supplies by mail order:

American Handicrafts
2617 W Seventh Street
Fort Worth, Texas 76707

**The Counting House at the
Hammock Shop**
Box 155
Pawleys Island
So. Carolina 29585

Economy Handicrafts
50–21 69th Street
Woodside
New York 11377

The Hidden Village
215 Yale Avenue
Claremont
California 91711

Lee Wards
Elgin
Illinois 60120

INDEX

Acknowledgments

The publishers would like to thank the following for kindly lending work to be photographed:

Joan Attewell: Landscape Panels 34.
Annie Corey: Christening Gown and Bonnet 66.
Christina Eustace: Swedish Cushion Cover 54.
Jacqueline Fancett: Sampler 54.
Susan Herbet: Pincushion 62.
Joyce Law: Beaded Combs 42.
Marti Murchison: 'Summer Beehive' and 'Herbaceous Border' pictures 58.
Anne Scott: Chevron Cushion Cover 46; Drawn Thread Skirt 70.
Susan Skeen: Purple Check Cushion Cover 74.
Deborah Suter: Cut Work Collar 70.
Tryphena Turner: Table Napkins 62.
Lois Vickers: 'Cottage Chrysanthemums' picture 38.
Angela Woodget: Beaded Jacket 42.

The publishers would also like to thank the following organizations for the loan of the items used in photography:

Royal School of Needlework: title page (embroidery frame); pages 10—11 (all materials and equipment).
Laura Ashley: title page (blouse and skirt); page 67 (cushion covers).
Wooden Heart: page 54 (chair).
The Reject Shop: page 71 (basket).
Adrian Mann: page 71 (jewellery).

Stitch illustrations by **Gerald Larn**
Other illustrations by **Carol Swatton, John Hutchinson, Terry Evans**.
Photographic styling by **Margaret Colvin**

All photography by **Steve Bicknell**, except Bridgeman Art Library 7, 8; E. T. Archive 9; National Portrait Gallery 6.

BACKGROUND PHOTOGRAPHY: REX BAMBER
FRONT PANEL PHOTOGRAPHY: ROBERT BELTON
BACK PANEL PHOTOGRAPHY: STEVE BICKNELL

How Are You Feeling Today?

Molly Potter

ILLUSTRATED BY Sarah Jennings

FEATHERSTONE
AN IMPRINT OF BLOOMSBURY
LONDON OXFORD NEW YORK NEW DELHI SYDNEY

For Caroline, who is very good at emotions.

Featherstone
An imprint of Bloomsbury Publishing Plc

50 Bedford Square
London
WC1B 3DP
UK

1385 Broadway
New York
NY 10018
USA

www.bloomsbury.com

FEATHERSTONE and the Feather logo are trademarks of Bloomsbury Publishing Plc

First published in 2014
Text copyright © Molly Potter, 2014
Illustrations copyright © Sarah Jennings, 2014

Molly Potter has asserted her right under the Copyright, Designs and Patents Act, 1988, to be identified as Author of this work.

All rights reserved. No part of this publication may be reproduced or transmitted in any form or by any means, electronic or mechanical, including photocopying, recording, or any information storage or retrieval system, without prior permission in writing from the publishers.

A catalogue record for this book is available from the British Library.

Library of Congress Cataloguing-in-Publication data has been applied for.

ISBN

HB: 978-1-4729-0609-0
ePDF: 978-1-4729-0736-3
ePUB: 978-1-4729-6186-0

18

Printed and bound in China by Leo Paper Products, Heshan, Guangdong

This book is produced using paper that is made from wood grown in managed, sustainable forests. It is natural, renewable and recyclable. The logging and manufacturing processes conform to the environmental regulations of the country of origin.

To find out more about our authors and books visit www.bloomsbury.com. Here you will find extracts, author interviews, details of forthcoming events and the option to sign up for our newsletters.

How are you feeling today?

Everything we do and and every thought we have comes with a feeling. Sometimes those feelings feel good and sometimes they feel nasty.

Some feelings are strong and some feelings are weak. We hardly notice the weak ones. When we feel something, we can choose what to do about that feeling. Sometimes we decide to ignore it and it goes away, but other times it takes over and we cannot think about anything else.

When you get a feeling, first work out what it is and then dip into this book for some ideas about what to do with that feeling. It will help you get to know your feelings better!

If you are feeling...

happy...

turn to page 6.

angry...

turn to page 8.

bored...

turn to page 10.

worried...

turn to page 12.

sad...

turn to page 14.

excited...

turn to page 16.

4

. . . grumpy

turn to page 18.

. . . scared

turn to page 20.

. . . quiet

turn to page 22.

. . . jealous

turn to page 24.

. . . embarrassed

turn to page 26.

. . . shy

turn to page 28.

When you feel happy, you could . . .

See if you can make yourself laugh. Start by pretending and see if it becomes real. You might get some funny looks!

Ha ha ha ha!

Make a list or draw pictures of food, people, places and other things that make you happy – like eating chocolate cake or flying a kite!

Make someone else happy by telling them how special they are.

Hum, whistle or sing at the top of your voice.

Hmm... ...mmm!

Decide what happiness looks, sounds, tastes, smells and feels like. Imagine yourself eating or cuddling happiness!

Make a happy collection – a box of things that make you happy. Include photos and nice things people have said to you.

Skip around and make everyone wonder why you are so happy!

Make a smile collage. Cut out smiles from magazines and stick them on a large piece of paper. Draw some, too!

Feeling happy is a nice feeling. It makes you smile and feel like the world is a wonderful place.

When you feel angry, you could . . .

Curl up into an ever-so-little ball, frown and grit your teeth.

Draw lots and lots of clouds to help the anger float away.

Run super-fast on the spot until you are really worn out.

Hit a pillow (but not too hard!).

Tell yourself 'I will be OK' over and over again until you believe it.

Close your eyes and take some deep, deep breaths.

Go for a walk in the garden or the park.

Count down from 100. Try not to fall asleep!

Feeling angry or cross usually feels quite horrible. It can sometimes make you want to bash things but this is never a good idea because other people get hurt and things get damaged!

When you feel **bored**, you could . . .

Sit still, rest and imagine yourself on a hot, sunny beach eating a yummy ice cream.

Find someone and challenge them to a tickle fight and get giggling!

Tidy up a messy drawer or a jumbled shelf.

Wander around trying to find every letter of the alphabet in your house somewhere.

Look at some old photos and see how you have changed.

Listen to some lively music and get jiggling to it!

Try and copy a picture from a book that you like.

Explore your house and garden looking for the five absolutely nicest places to be.

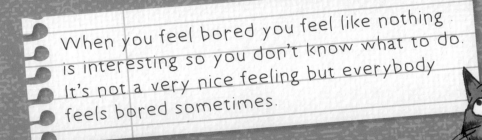

When you feel bored you feel like nothing is interesting so you don't know what to do. It's not a very nice feeling but everybody feels bored sometimes.

11

When you feel **worried**, you could . . .

Find someone you trust and tell them about all of your worries.

Imagine a giant machine sucking the worry completely out of you.

Picture the worry in a bubble and blow it away high into the sky.

Watch a film or TV programme you know you really enjoy and concentrate on nothing else.

Think of a funny or silly tune playing in the place where you feel worried.

Take lots of really deep, deep breaths.

Imagine yourself floating on some calm, clear blue water.

Imagine yourself much, much bigger than the thing you are worrying about.

They are tiny.

Feeling worried is not a nice feeling. It usually happens when we think an unhelpful thought over and over again about something that might happen in the future.

When you feel sad, you could...

Find someone who usually makes you happy and sit next to them.

Find a cosy and comfortable place and have a really big cry.

Do something kind for someone else.

Daydream about something you are looking forward to.

Do some star jumps until you are out of breath and worn out.

Dance in a silly way to some cheerful music.

Find a place to sit and quietly watch your thoughts pass by.

Imagine yourself laughing your head off.

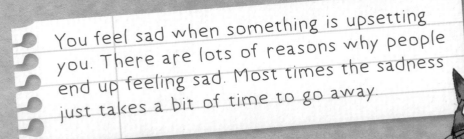

You feel sad when something is upsetting you. There are lots of reasons why people end up feeling sad. Most times the sadness just takes a bit of time to go away.

When you feel **excited**, you could . . .

Say 'yippee' and 'yeh' in your squeakiest voice.

Think about your tummy and decide whether it feels more like there are butterflies, fireworks or popping bubbles inside it.

Do a beaming smile and show those teeth!

Tell someone exactly why you are so excited.

Make up an excitement dance using just your hands.

Jump as high as you possibly can until you feel like you can reach the sky!

Clap your hands super quickly.

Draw a picture of what you think excitement looks like (if you can stay still long enough!).

Feeling excited can be a great feeling. It usually happens when you are really, really looking forward to something or really, really enjoying something.

If you feel grumpy, you could . . .

Sit really still and stare at a blank wall.

Do something easy-peasy that you know you love doing.

I feel better already.

Go outside. Close your eyes tight. Face the wind and feel it on your face.

Sit and sulk in a nice corner and if anyone asks, say, 'I am sulking in the corner' and smile!

Huff and puff, tut and roll your eyes over and over again – it might make you laugh.

Imagine you are a grumpy monster and a wizard comes along, waves his wand and turns you into a huge, fluffy smiley monster that gives presents to everyone.

Go and lie in bed, shut your eyes and imagine having a bath in jelly.

I AM GRUMPY
I am grumpy
I AM GRUMPY I am grumpy
I am grumpy

Try saying 'I am grumpy' in lots and lots of different voices.

Feeling grumpy is not nice. You are grumpy when you get easily annoyed – possibly because you are tired or having to do something you don't like.

19

If you feel scared, you could . . .

Run really, really fast and get away from any danger as quickly as possible.

Shout and scream extra loud for help.

Say very clearly that you are scared.

Shut your eyes tight if it helps.

Laugh and point at scary things.

Imagine the thing that is scaring you being tiny enough to fit in your hand.

Think about the time when the scary thing will be over and you are no longer scared.

Imagine yourself eating a giant pudding with a teaspoon.

People feel scared when they are in danger or when they are unsure about doing something they haven't done before.

When you feel like you want to be quiet ...

Have a hot and soothing bubble bath.

Go outside and breathe in the fresh air.

Go looking for the quietest place in your house and sit in it.

Drink a hot drink that you love and let the drink warm your hands.

22

Imagine a beautiful, blue butterfly
fluttering past.

Chat quietly to your pet if you have one.

I'm having
a quiet day
today.

Tell people you are feeling really quiet
and don't feel like noisiness.

Lie on your bed and stare at the clouds
out of the window.

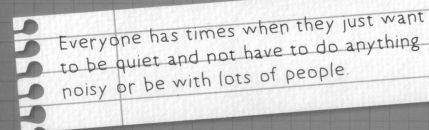

Everyone has times when they just want
to be quiet and not have to do anything
noisy or be with lots of people.

When you feel jealous or envious, you could . . .

Go to your room and look at all the wonderful things you have.

Find someone you love being with and ask them to say something nice to you.

Practise giving other people praise and compliments when they do things well.

Smile for exactly one minute.

Try to enjoy and celebrate when other people succeed.

Say 'well done' or 'you're lucky' when people do well.

Think of yourself as lucky – there are always people worse off than you.

Imagine yourself as a rich king or queen.

Feeling jealous or envious happens when we want what someone else has or we feel someone wants to be with another person more than they want to be with us.

When you feel embarrassed, you could . . .

Make yourself as busy as a bee.

Remember every single person will soon forget what happened.

Laugh loudly at yourself and smile at how silly you have been.

Learn from what you did so you don't do it again.

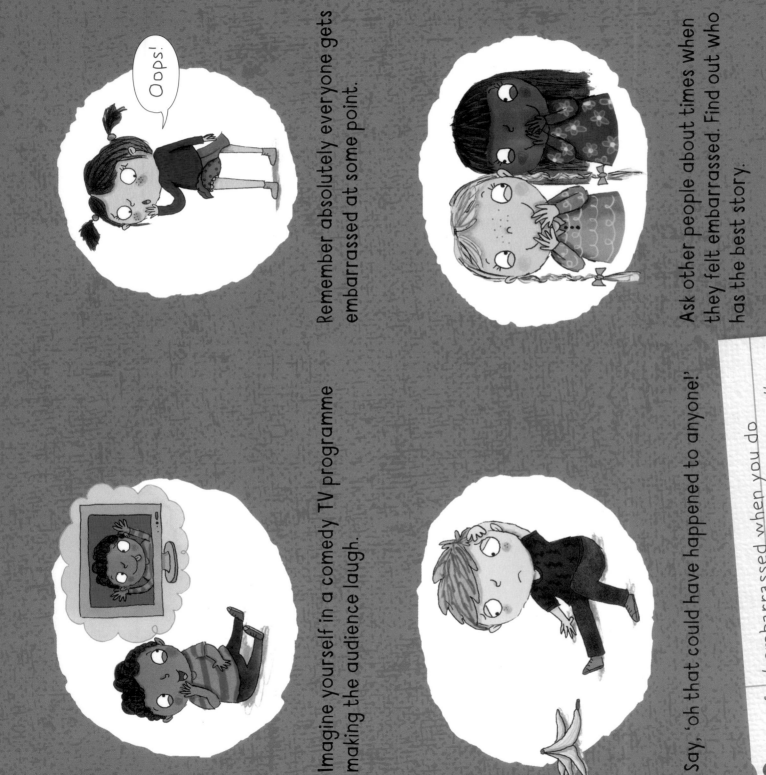

"Oops!"

Imagine yourself in a comedy TV programme making the audience laugh.

Remember absolutely everyone gets embarrassed at some point.

Ask other people about times when they felt embarrassed. Find out who has the best story.

Say, 'oh that could have happened to anyone!'

You feel embarrassed when you do something you think made you look silly or stupid. Being embarrassed can make you go bright red in the face.

27

When you feel shy, you could . . .

Tell yourself it's totally OK to be a quiet person.

Imagine that everyone feels just the same way as you do.

Know that most people feel shy at some time.

Be brave, smile and say a cheerful 'hello'.

Stand next to the people you know well when you are meeting new people.

Think of a simple question to ask someone.

Talk about something you love to do.

Build up to giving someone a compliment.

Feeling shy is when you feel a little bit scared or awkward around people. You are most likely to feel shy when you meet new people.

29

Emotional literacy – a brief guide for parents

What is emotional literacy?

You might have heard the term 'emotional literacy' used at your child's school and wondered what it meant. It is best explained by looking at what a child with emotional literacy is like.

A child who is emotionally literate…

• is aware of and can usually name or explain the feelings they are experiencing.
• can usually understand what caused the feeling.
• knows the best way to behave to deal with the feeling.
• can take other people's feeling into account in any situation.

Why is emotional literacy important?

Anyone who has tried to think clearly when they are really angry will understand the power emotions can have over us. Emotions are an unavoidable part of being human and they need not be a problem if we have the tools to allow them to leave nearly as easily as they arrive. Healthy emotions 'flow' backwards and forwards and don't get stuck.

Emotions are very real and it's unhealthy to pretend they don't exist or affect our children. It's how children learn to manage these inevitable feelings that has a huge impact on their lives.

Children who can process their feelings well…

• build and maintain healthy relationships.
• communicate positively and not defensively.
• deal with challenges in a more positive and less anxious way.
• have less stress.
• get more out of life.

If children cannot process their feelings successfully they become 'stuck' and every time they are in a similar situation they will respond by experiencing the same emotion. That situation will therefore always be a trigger for that emotion. For example, if a child always feels shame when they are asked to read because they struggle with reading, and this emotion is not helpfully processed, the child will always connect reading with a negative emotion.

What are signs of poor emotional literacy?

When a child hasn't learnt how to manage their emotions well they…
• cannot describe how they are feeling.
• rarely talk about their emotions.
• don't ask for and don't expect help when they are feeling bad.
• express their emotions in unhelpful ways – for example, hitting, shouting or sulking.
• don't consciously recognise that emotions have got the better of them.

Emotional literacy for boys

Talking about feelings is not just for girls. In fact, because girls are generally encouraged to be more open about feelings, they tend to need less support. Boys are expected to be 'strong' and sadly, this often means they get the message that the only acceptable emotion to show is anger. This can leave boys feeling very emotionally 'stuck', which is not healthy.

How can I help my child to manage their feelings well?

Young children need to learn how to manage their feelings in a healthy way and they learn this mostly from the key adults in their lives. Helping your child become emotionally literate involves:

1. Acknowledging feelings

Ignoring or denying how your child feels will cause further upset. Children can't help the emotions they feel and they are completely real for them – as they are for adults. Acknowledge feelings using statements like. 'I can see you are angry,' or 'I would feel sad too if that happened to me.'

2. Talking about feelings

Talk to your child about how they are feeling and ask questions such as:

* What happened to cause this feeling?
* Can you describe the feeling?
* Would you feel the same way if this had happened to you?
* Which kind of situations make you feel happy, angry, sad, excited etc?

3. Helping your child understand the choices they have when they feel a particular emotion

A child cannot help feeling angry, worried, scared or upset, but they do have a choice about what action to take or how to behave. This book suggests some good choices for different emotions.

Help your child to see that there are unhelpful things to do when they feel sad, for example sulking, moaning or making someone else feel sad, and there are helpful things like talking to someone, finding something to do that comforts them or finding out if they can do something about the situation.

feelings are feelings
(they cannot be denied)
BUT
you do have a
CHOICE
about how
you behave
BEHAVE   BEHAVE

BEHAVE
when you are taken over by
a difficult emotion

4. Helping your child to imagine what other people might be feeling (developing empathy)

A child that can imagine what it is like to be in another person's shoes is more likely to respond helpfully to situations with uncomfortable feelings, be better at making friends and more likely to be happy.

Help your child develop empathy by using stories, pictures, TV dramas or real life situations to talk about how people are probably feeling. Encourage younger children to 'read' other people's faces and decide what they might be feeling.

What other ideas can I use to help my child manage his or her feelings?

See behaviour as a clue

When your child sulks, or shouts, or goes quietly to his or her room, they are communicating a feeling through their behaviour. These can be opportunities to open up a conversation about feelings. You can start by guessing what they might be feeling and why they might be feeling that way.

Picture tools

There are a variety of posters and picture tools (including this book) that could be used to help your child recognise and understand difficult emotions.

Feeling tracker (see next page)

If your child has had a difficult day, this tracker could be used to help them reflect upon what happened and what made them feel bad and what made them feel good. Ask your child to think back on a day and draw a line graph. For positive emotions they draw a line in the upper section of the graph and for negative emotions the lower section of the graph. They can then label what caused the emotional changes throughout the day and their related feelings can be discussed.

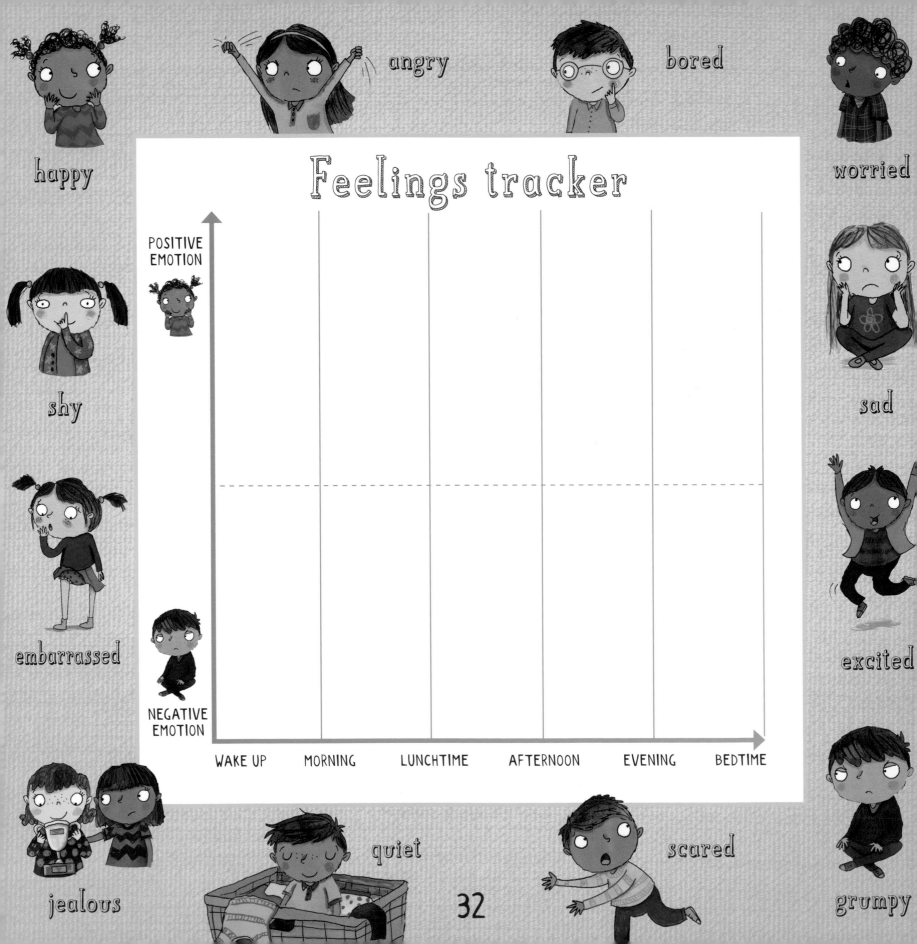

happy

angry

bored

worried

shy

sad

embarrassed

excited

jealous

quiet

scared

grumpy

Feelings tracker

POSITIVE
EMOTION

NEGATIVE
EMOTION

WAKE UP   MORNING   LUNCHTIME   AFTERNOON   EVENING   BEDTIME

32